And I Know
Too Much to Pretend

~ A Memoir ~

Lorraine M. Duvall

D1596264

Bloated Toe Publishing
Peru, New York

I cling to the conviction that there is some
organic thread to the things that happen to us,
which lurks patiently in experience,
hoping to be found out.

—Phillip Lopate, *To Show and to Tell*

© 2014 by Lorraine M. Duvall

And I Know Too Much to Pretend

~ A Memoir ~

First Edition

Library of Congress Control Number: 2014940361

ISBN-13: 978-1-939216-35-9   ISBN-10: 1-939216-35-4

Visit the author at
www.loradk.com

Visit the Bloated Toe Publishing website:
www.bloatedtoe.com   info@bloatedtoe.com

Photo in Epilogue, p.165, courtesy of the Albany Times Union

Covers designed by Lorraine M. Duvall,
created by Jill C. Jones and Lawrence P. Gooley of Bloated Toe Publishing

Printed and bound by
Versa Press, 1465 Spring Bay Road, East Peoria, IL 61611-9788

Manufactured in the United States of America

Contents

Prologue

Recently, a tiny scenario in my life illustrated the point I want to make in this book—a simple point really, but one that has profound implications for every woman. That is, every woman who believes in having the power to make choices for herself.

Lake Placid, a village in the Adirondack Mountains near my home, hosts a series of six classical music concerts every summer. Bruce and I bought season tickets last summer. At the first concert, I noticed about seven or eight rows in front of our seats a tall man and a petite woman sitting next to each other on the side aisle. He had a clear view of the orchestra; she sat behind a man who was not only tall but heavy, blocking her view of the stage.

At the first concert I thought to myself, Why doesn't she move? There are plenty of empty seats in their row. If she just moved two seats to her right she would have a clear view of the orchestra. I was perplexed.

My frustration grew at subsequent concerts as this woman sat careening her head around this barrier of a man in front of her to try to see the orchestra. I wanted to go up to her and say, Why don't you move your seat so you can enjoy the concert?

I see some choices she could have made:

- Stay where she was and passively try to overcome the obstacle.
- Stay where she was and resent being placed in the situation.
- Ask her husband to change seats with her or to change both of their seats.
- Take charge and change both of their seats.
- Take charge and move to a seat of her choice.

I found myself ruminating on how this situation illustrates the way one woman viewed her role in her relationship, and perhaps, reflects women's role in our society.

This book is for women who want to choose their own seats, to take charge of their lives, because the choices we make, even at the smallest levels, slowly, gradually open out into the lives we live. To me, every decision is that important.

I now see, in hindsight, I made my choices because I wanted to be a woman who lived outside preset choices—choices for women made by others in the years while I was coming to maturity—and even after, when I was an adult woman who should have been able to make choices for myself. The choices made for women in those times—in dress, career, partnering—seemed to me confining and soul-deadening.

Early in life I tried on some of those choices, only to find they were, for me, ill-fitting. While other women found themselves and their happiness in what we might call more traditional roles for women, I did not.

My soul was restless as far back as I can remember. Something in me longed to explore the freer spaces of life and the world. While I was in many ways quieter, and in that sense more contained, than other girls and women when it came to being outwardly expressive, inwardly I yearned to pursue a life outside the norm. Fortunately, a few—a very few—women were there to awaken my soul to other possibilities beyond the preset limits of choices girls and women could make.

Luckily, as well, I encountered them early.

I was born in 1938 to a middle-class family and grew up in a mid-size town in upstate New York. I struggled through the feminist revolution, which for me meant finding my way as an independent woman, not wanting to play the role of a conventional housewife, forging a career through problematic times. I opened my heart and soul to Eastern mystical practices that helped me to live a joyful adult life.

I made choices, sometimes challenging, leading towards

unknown territory. Think of the children's book series, *Choose Your Own Adventure*, where the readers are warned,

> From time to time as you read along, you will be asked to make a choice. Your choice may lead to a successful journey or a disaster. The adventures you have are the results of your choices. You are responsible because you choose.[1]

At times we change our seats to survive. Better yet, we change our seats to thrive.

Part I

Planting the Seeds

The Beginning

Because they have so little, children must rely
on imagination rather than experience.
—Eleanor Roosevelt, *You Learn by Living*

"Lorraine, where are you?" my mother shouted.

She was standing on the back stoop of our house located in a middle-class neighborhood in Binghamton, New York. "Are you hiding again?" She never seemed to recognize my need to be alone, forgetting that, after all, I had two sisters around most of the time. "Keep an eye on your younger sister," my mother often requested. I just wanted to have the freedom to pursue my own interests, especially since I was six and could venture around the neighborhood by myself.

There were scores of neighborhood kids my age. I enjoyed playing games with them, but sometimes I needed to be alone. That's when I went to the bush behind my house. I'd crawl under the forsythia that grew just beyond the stairs that led to our back porch. I liked it best when the bottom branches had been trimmed enough to allow me to sit upright on the dirt floor, hidden from the rest of the world by the mature branches overhead.

Sitting here quietly, I created my own world. The larger rocks represented parents; the smaller rocks the kids; the pebbles the babies. Sometimes the kids left home and got into mischief. I liked to pretend I was one of those kids who could do whatever they wanted to do when they wanted to do it—sleep late, go to the store and buy candy, sit and play with their dolls, alone.

I don't know where this need came from, to be independent even as a small child. I just know I yearned to be free—to not have to conform to what all the other kids were doing.

I wanted choices. And I wanted to be free to make my own choices.

Sometimes my friend Maggie Hawkins and I played hopscotch on our driveway—sometimes on her driveway, as only about a foot of grass separated the two. I liked Maggie, and her mother fascinated me.

Mrs. Hawkins seemed different than the other moms, even my mom. I noticed that she did not spend time with the other moms and would drive off in their car alone. I'd wonder where she went. "Where is your mom going?" I'd ask Maggie. She usually did not know, which left me imagining what the world was like outside of my neighborhood that Mrs. Hawkins was exploring.

One day after a rain, I watched Mrs. Hawkins standing on their

Sisters: Harriet, Lorraine, and Vivian

back porch, looking with a faraway gaze at a beautiful rainbow that had appeared—and not just looking, but singing, "Somewhere, Over the Rainbow."

I couldn't stop watching Mrs. Hawkins's face silhouetted against the sky while she sang about birds flying away and wishing on a star. I had learned to do that—wish upon a star—but here was a mother singing about it, out loud, in our neighborhood.

It was clear that a part of her wanted to be elsewhere.

I suppose that somewhere inside, I was aware that people in my neighborhood might think a lot of things about singing out loud for all to hear. And all of them would lead to the conclusion: This is something you just don't do.

This, after all, was the very conservative, conformed 1940s. In my sheltered world, women stayed inside their homes, cooking, cleaning, sewing, taking care of children and husbands ... *not* singing on the back stoop.[2]

I did not realize at the time why I was so intrigued by Mrs. Hawkins' behavior. I just knew she was different than the other moms.

I noticed Mrs. Hawkins because she did not act like she cared about keeping their house clean. She wasn't busy like my mother. She did not discipline Maggie like we were disciplined. Maggie seemed to have much more freedom than my sisters and me. Sometimes Maggie could stay and finish a game we were playing before she had to go and eat lunch or dinner. We always had to stop what we were doing and go when called.

Maggie was given more freedom than my mother allowed us. She could be called Maggie instead of Margaret, another example of how our mothers differed. My mother insisted we be called the names she had given us—Vivian, Lorraine, and Harriet. "If I wanted people to call you *Lori* I would have named you *Lori!* Your name is *Lorraine*," my mother often said, when friends tried to shorten my name. Much to her annoyance, kids often called my sisters Vivie and Hattie. I wanted our friends to have the choice to call us what they wanted to call us.

Mrs. Hawkins seemed softer, like a precursor to a '60s hippie, the kind of woman called a "flower child." She later became a professor of English Literature.

Even at such a young age, hearing her sing, I felt a longing in her that touched my longing. A longing to be free to discover.

As I got older, I continued to take advantage of ways of using my imagination to explore my inner and outer worlds.

I often went into the woods alone during my grade-school years. I could do that because we spent every summer at a cottage my parents bought in 1946 on Quaker Lake, just south of Binghamton, over the border in Pennsylvania. My father commuted the 15 miles to Binghamton while my two sisters and I stayed at the Lake with my mother.

"Mom, I'm going to walk out to the stone fence—be back in a little while," I'd say, stretching the truth somewhat. Although the woods in the back of our cottage did contain some stone fences made years ago when the land was farmed, my destination was a special area among the trees, known only to me.

I constructed the layout of a house in a part of the woods, using existing trees to outline the rooms. I moved branches to imitate furniture, and made use of the forest moss for my bed.

I'm home now, I said to myself as I walked through a column of trees, imagining a front foyer. I ate lunch with twig utensils and slept in my moss bed. My wild world was my own.

I loved playing in the water at Quaker Lake.

I'd swim with a rubber tube (taken from a truck tire) far enough away from the dock so no one could hear me talking to my imaginary friends, the maple leaves. In the water, my leaf friends and I would bob along and flow with the gentle waves. If the waves were too intense we would find shelter in

Lorraine

the center of the tube, which sometimes took a lot of strength, as we had to dive under or climb over the tube ring to get to the center.

Swimming with the family at Quaker Lake

- - - - -

The adolescent years presented their own challenges.

My Best Friend Pam

It takes courage to grow up and become who you really are.
—e. e. cummings

"There's a new girl in the neighborhood. She and her mother are coming over this afternoon so you can meet her. Her name is Pam," my mother said one day after I returned from school.

Maggie and her family had just moved away, so I was happy to have a new girl my age in the neighborhood. Pam and I hit it off right away, becoming the best of friends.

Pam's house was just around the corner. A quicker way to go from her house to mine was through a 20-foot-long, 5-foot-wide path that separated our garage from Maggie's garage, ending up at the end of Pam's driveway and the entrance to their garage.

During the day and night, Pam and I hurried between our homes, using the 20-foot path rather than walk around the corner. We'd hurry, as it was scary—dark even when the sun lit up either entrance. The roofs of both garages almost touched, allowing very little light to shine through. At night we could hardly see the light on either end.

"Pam ... Lorraine" we'd yell to each other repeatedly until Pam got to the other side. Thankfully for me, Pam usually came to my house and I did not have to go through the path alone. Sometimes when I would go to her house, we'd play croquet on the side lawn or badminton on the yard on the other side of the house. Her yard was much bigger than ours.

Pam's house looked fancier than ours, with large stones on the outside and two living rooms, one on each side after you entered through the front door. I never knew how her mother decided which living room to use.

I always entered through the back of the house to the kitchen and its pantry. "Be quiet. My Dad is home," Pam often whispered when I came over.

Her father scared me. He worked out of an office in their large house. He never talked to me, and spoke to Pam in a loud voice. That was a lot different than my father, who engaged us in his life and joked around with my mother and my two sisters and me.

When we hit puberty, our friendship ripened into a type of bond. Pam and I made a pact: we would encourage each other to take bold actions.

Our first bold action was to confront our mothers.

"Tomorrow we will ask our Moms to buy us bras," we vowed one night.

We were the only two of our girlfriends who were not wearing them. Pam and I felt out of place. Wearing a bra was a right-of-passage in those days, whether needed or not.

My mother didn't talk to me and my sisters about personal matters. "Don't cry, don't be a baby," she admonished us if we became emotional. I felt courageous asking my mother about anything related to what was happening to my body since she seemed just as embarrassed as I was to discuss puberty issues. She never spoke about menstruation. One day she handed me the booklet "Growing Up And Liking It," published by Modess, a manufacturer of sanitary napkins.

Sharing this pamphlet with Pam, we learned not only about menstrual periods and related hygiene, but what was happening with boys, a subject foreign to us. I had no brothers. Pam had three older brothers who were in their own worlds. Certainly we never talked to boys our age about anything personal.

Ours was an innocent time. Or maybe "a time when nothing was talked about" is more accurate.

- - - - -

I didn't talk about my imaginary world—how I wished I had the power of the comic strip heroine Scarlet O'Neil to become invisible by touching my left wrist.[3] If I became invisible, I reasoned, I could go and do the things I wanted, without feeling judged. I could pursue adventures like Nancy Drew in her role as a self-assured private detective.

But I was afraid to venture outside the norm. My need to be loved and accepted led me to try to be more like Doris Day.

I looked at the movie actress Doris Day as the pure, happy-go-lucky girl we all wanted to be, singing songs like "By the Light of the Silvery Moon" or "Aba Daba Honeymoon" by Theresa Brewer. I imagined dancing with Fred Astaire. Glenn Ford was my favorite actor. He looked somewhat like my father.

I liked thinking about this fantasy world when trying to emulate the popular girls in the school, mostly admiring their clothes. As is true with many adolescents, the pull to emulate was very powerful.

We wore skirts except for sports, and in the summer when culottes and shorts were acceptable. We never wore slacks to school, always mid-calf length skirts and oxfords—except for special occasions, when we dressed up with starched crinolines that puffed out our wide skirts.

Suzanne's mother made felt skirts for a few of us, embroidered with multiple colored cutouts of poodles.

Our other friends were jealous of these "unique" outfits—at least that's how we saw them. As unique. Not just the new conformity they really were.

For church and other dress-up occasions, we begged our mothers to buy us Lanz dresses and Capezio flats. One day my mother took me to the best clothing store in Binghamton, Drazens, and bought me an expensive skirt and blouse outfit with horizontal stripes, justifying the cost by saying I needed the stripes to make me look heavier—I was tall and skinny, a look that was frowned upon then. Women were supposed to have curves to make them look sexy.

- - - - -

One minor rebellion from the norms of the day came in the form of singing wicked songs:

Brassiere ...
Hanging from the chandelier
How much we want you near
Brassiere

We'd sing this with our girlfriends, giggling at our daring (hoping no one else would hear us).

Pam led us in a number of adventures that took us further into the exploratory world of puberty. One day we met at our friend Helen's house, in a loft above her garage. We went to the loft often because it offered us privacy from adult intrusion.

Pam giggled. "We'll take our shirts off all at the same time so nobody will chicken-out. Then our pants."

We wanted to see what other girls looked like during this trying period of significant bodily changes. And it felt daring. I was *in*.

When the courageous deed was done, we sheepishly looked at each other. Some talked about their body. I was too shy.

Anything having to do with our growing sexuality bothered me.

One day Pam and I went to the house of a friend who had a dog. Shortly after we entered the living room, this small white terrier climbed his front paws up my leg and, powered by his hind paws, rhythmically moved his body up and down my leg.

Pointing at me and laughing, our friend said, "My dog is trying to have sex with you!" After I kicked my leg and pushed the dog away, she made matters more embarrassing. "We'll call you S. L. for <u>S</u>exy <u>L</u>eg," she shouted to the others in the living room. As the story spread, more and more of my classmates taunted me by yelling, "There is S. L." as I walked down the hall in school. Pam, understanding my humiliation, would stick up for me, explaining, "It means Spider Legs because her legs are so skinny." And my legs were skinny, so the cover-up worked.

By choice, Pam was my best friend because she was an explorer.

- - - - -

We continued our explorations in nudity one summer at a deserted pond in the Adirondack Mountains. "Let's go skinny dipping," Pam challenged.

The summer of 1949, I followed Pam on a two-week canoe trip sponsored by the Girl Scout Camp Amahami, located about 50 miles from Binghamton, near Deposit, New York. Pam went there every summer for four weeks while I spent the two months of my vacation at our cottage on Quaker Lake. Sometimes she stayed with me at the lake before or after camp.

"We spend just one week at the camp practicing our canoe skills, then we go to the Adirondacks for a week of canoeing on the lakes," Pam offered as a way to encourage me to join her.

Canoeing in the Adirondacks

Ten of us campers along with two counselors and a trailer of canoes drove north for about five hours, spending four nights at a public campsite on the shores of Upper Saranac Lake, in the northern part of the Adirondack Park. We paddled around the lake for four days, exploring a portion of its islands, and small streams leading to other lakes and ponds.

Exploring a narrow stream led us to Sandy Pond, deserted enough that we dared to take off our bathing suits and swim nude. I experienced a freedom and an acceptance of my maturing body as the water flowed freely over my skin in the clear water of the pond, until Pam yelled, "There are people walking down the path toward our beach!" My shyness returned as I scurried to cover my body once again with a bathing suit.

The feeling of freedom I experienced at Sandy Pond stayed with me for years, reminding me that being in the wilderness opened something in me that I aspired to explore.

I felt a connection to the Adirondacks during this canoe trip, skinny-dipping on a remote, clear, spring-fed lake surrounded by mountains and trees, exploring the waters around the Saranac Lakes. I could not explain at this early age this link I felt to the Adirondacks. I just knew being there, I had similar feelings of when

I was playing in the bush behind my house, and the woods in the back of our cottage at Quaker Lake.

To help with my inner exploration, I was discovering an empowerment being aligned with girls who pushed what we thought was the norm of adolescent life, usually with Pam at the helm. We had fun in our Girl Scout troop in Binghamton.

Many of my friends were in the same troop, which was divided into four separate groups of girls. Pam and I were in the same group along with four other friends. Thinking we were really clever, we named our group WTWAC, and sang it to the tune of the Toreador's song from *Carmen*:

> WTWAC
> WTWAC
> WTWAC
> WTWAC

We tried to keep secret the meaning of the initials: We Think We Are Cute.

Finally, though, one of the other four in the group told on us and we were made fun of by others in the scout troop.

We did think we were cute. More important, we were distinguishing ourselves from the rest of the girls in our Girl Scout troop. Hanging out with girls who tried different things enabled me to have confidence in exploring my own individuality. They gave me strength. And humor.

We had jokes we told in front of boys and our families.

> QUESTION: What time is it?
> ANSWER: 2:30.
> RETORT: Why don't you go to the dentist?
> EXPLANATION (if needed): Tooth hurty.

Our cleverness knew no bounds.

Pam, a competent athlete, was always careful to watch her weight and strove to master the skills needed in any sport, water

Our Girl Scout troop. Pam is in the bottom row, second from
the right. Lorraine is in the middle row, third from the right.

sports included. We laughed as she practiced her approach to a dive
not even close to a lake and a diving board, slowing picking up
speed as she placed one foot in front of the other while her hands
circled to meet at the top of her head, jumping as her arms swung in
front as if she were on a diving board.

Her interest in sports resulted in encouraging us to take part
in athletics in Junior High School. We played girls' intramural
volleyball, field hockey, and soccer. We took gymnastics classes
together. Most activities were really fun, except for a Slimnastics
class held early in the morning before school started. I went because
Pam wanted to go, even though I was a really skinny kid. After all,
we walked to school together every day. If I did not go, I'd be alone
walking to school on those mornings.

And while I enjoyed the camaraderie and Pam's cleverness,
there was an issue I did not see.

Someone else did.

Our gym teacher, Mrs. Holmes, took great interest in us girls, understanding that developing into healthy women involved more than active participation in physical sports.

"Please come to my office after the soccer practice today," Mrs. Holmes told me.

I was afraid I had done something wrong, and told Pam and our other friends that I had this meeting with our gym teacher.

Much to my surprise, when I went to her office, Mrs. Holmes kindly asked me to sit down in a chair next to her desk. With a soft voice she said, "I have noticed you hang out with Pam a lot. I worry that you follow her lead much of the time and do not show your personality."

No adult, not even my Mom, had ever talked to me in such a personal way. I just sat there quietly, red in the face, listening as she went, on giving me examples of what she had observed. "I'm concerned that Pam's influence keeps you from being yourself. You are much better at sports than you think. You are a smart girl and have lots of potential."

My shyness kept me from saying anything but "Thank you." I knew, however, that what she said was the truth—I needed to regain that independence I felt years before as a child playing in the woods, on the water—to explore Mrs. Hawkins' rainbow.

I left the meeting not knowing what to say to my friends. I knew this conversation should stay between Mrs. Holmes and me.

"What did Mrs. Holmes say?" Pam asked as we walked home from school that day.

"Nothing much," I mumbled. The advice Mrs. Holmes gave me was just sinking in. I did follow Pam around a lot. I thought, Pam is fun. I like being with her. She is my best friend. As a shy person, being with Pam gave me courage to do things I might not do otherwise. I knew everyone liked Pam, and possibly, if I hung around with her, people would like me, too.

Thanks to the light Mrs. Holmes shone on me that day, I began to be aware of how I hid behind Pam's popularity. I started to follow my own interests. I was learning that, yes indeed, I was happier when I asserted myself and worried less what others thought of me.

This new assertiveness paid-off. In high school I became president of the Leaders Club and an editor of the student newspaper. I was proud of the nomination as a delegate of my high school to the Citizenship Conference at Syracuse University. Being highlighted as a "Super Senior" in the newspaper helped my confidence in putting myself forward. I could achieve. And people liked me.

Thank you, Mrs. Holmes.

Boys & Men

Donald James Duvall dies at the age of 49,
leaving a wife and three teenage daughters, ages 13, 15, and 17,
after battling stomach and esophageal cancer for six months.
—Binghamton Press, April 1954

I was the 15-year-old daughter. My mother was 46.

Vivian answered the phone. When I came into the room, we looked at each other, surmising the worst. Our mother was not home. We called her friends until we found her visiting neighbors after she had left the hospital.

"Should we wake Harriet and tell her?" my mother asked.

"Yes," I replied.

Our father was dead. We needed to be together.

My sisters and I had not been told my father had cancer until three days before he died. Cancer was considered a shameful disease.

I did not cry that night. I was still in disbelief, could not fathom what death really meant—that we would never have dinner again with my father. He would not be there to hear what we did in school, to joke with us when we were too serious.

On the first morning when my mother's friends came over, I stood in the dining room not knowing what to do. My friend Suzanne's mother crossed the room and hugged me—a surprise, for hugging was not an acceptable way of greeting in 1954. With that hug, however, I knew that people cared and we were not alone.

We had close ties to the Tabernacle Methodist Church community—my father was on the governing board, and we kids attended Sunday school and were members of choir and the youth group. Because of my parents' involvement in civic activities, my father's death was considered a community loss. We sisters had many friends. The community was there for us.

My mother kept her emotions in check, at least to us kids. Knowing we were on our own, she concentrated on our financial needs.

My father had had a successful career with Monroe Calculator Company, with not much life insurance and a pension that contained no benefits for a surviving spouse. Spousal benefits for pensions of deceased employees only became available in U.S. corporations ten and twenty years later.

The year before the doctors discovered the cancer, my mother talked my father out of spending money on more life insurance for him so we could take an extended automobile trip to California.

Now my mother needed to work. Only a small amount of money came to us kids from Social Security.

Only one mother in my neighborhood had a job—a neighborhood with modest homes, a middle-class section of the city, not even the best part of town. I remember feeling sorry for Kathy and Sara because they did not appear to have much money. Their Mom was a social worker. Most of the jobs for women in the post-World War II

My mother and father on our trip to California with the Packard convertible

era did not pay well—secretary, teacher, nurse, clerical worker, sales clerk, and social worker.

It stood out in my mind that our pediatrician was a woman. I admired that a woman could be in a profession that consisted mostly of men, especially a profession where you could make a lot of money. I also admired her because she used her maiden name in business and her married name socially. This was the first time I ever heard that a woman could keep her name. It caused me to think that a woman did have the *option* to live an independent, fulfilling life, even if married.

Working as a professional woman appealed to me much more than struggling along, working just to bring home an extra bit of money to contribute to the family budget, as so many women were forced to do.

Even with the loss of my father and the loss of his income, my mother was better off than most women her age, those who had been housewives all their lives with few skills that would help them gain meaningful employment.

My mother helped my father after he made a large sale of calculators. She conducted weeklong training sessions for client on how to most effectively utilize the machines for their business. I am not sure if she was ever paid for performing these services. She may have just done it to support my father.

Now our survival depended upon my mother's earning power. My father was the love of her life, but she had no interest in marrying, even if it meant the support of a man.

To ease the financial loss after my father's death, the Monroe Company loaned my mother eight to ten calculating machines so she could start her own business, Duvall Calculating and Figuring Services. She thought they loaned her the calculators to help relieve their guilt in not providing us with any financial assistance.

My mother built an office in our basement, hiring neighborhood women to work at peak times, usually in January and February when companies needed year-end inventories done. A woman-owned business was unusual in the 1950s, especially one not centered on fashion and female products.

I ran the calculators for $0.50 an hour.

I'd come home from high school with all these women working downstairs, diligently clanking away on the calculating machines until their afternoon break, when they'd come upstairs for their coffee and tea, chatting away. My home felt warm and comfortable when they were there. I felt protected.

Even without a father, my life remained stable during my high school years because of my mother's initiative and strength.

My friend Linda's mother was different from my mother—a lot different. When my friends and I went to Linda's house in junior high school, before her father died, her mother hugged us and laughed as she included us in her daily activities. I liked going to Linda's house, where I could relax and not have to always be on my best behavior. Here was the thing: Linda's mother expressed her emotions much more than my mother. Sometimes I wished my mother showed me the love Linda's mother showed her.

Linda's mother, however, was not as resilient as mine.

Life changed drastically for Linda in her sophomore year in high school, just as mine did. Her father died also. It was harder on Linda than me since her mother left Linda to care for her two younger siblings, a brother and a sister. Emotionally, her mother never was able to cope with the loss of her husband, and placed a huge burden on Linda during her high school and college years. She was never able to be a part of the world without her husband.

I felt fortunate because my mother continued to provide me with a role model I admired. She was a woman who could make it without a man if she had to.

"I have good news," my mother said, screaming over the phone, calling me at my college dorm in 1959. "Governor Nelson Rockefeller just appointed me to a posh position." This New York State appointment as a District Administrator of Workmen's Compensation Board that included the territory around Binghamton was not necessarily "posh," but did provide her with a better-than-average salary for women. She retired 12 years later with a good retirement package.

After taking this new position, my mother sold Duvall Inventory and Figuring Service to a woman who worked for her in the office in our basement.

As her daughter, the joy for me was seeing that my mother was given an opportunity to use her talents in a meaningful way and to become her own person in a man's world. She was the only women of ten administrators covering the state, and often hobnobbed with the governor and his staff.

I felt deeply grateful that my mother's response to my father's death provided me with a role model of strength and empowerment, pointing the way to a self-determined life. I saw that life could have been very different for my sisters and me if my mother had not taken charge.

All was not easy, however, primarily because of my older sister. I became the responsible child in the family when my parents visited the Lahey Clinic in Boston, where my father had an operation to remove the cancerous growth from his stomach.[4]

My mother with her board colleagues

My parents left me in charge of the household because of Vivian's rebellious teenage behavior consisting of not following their rules, like drinking with her friends at late-night parties. Naming me in charge caused my 17-year-old sister to resent her younger 15-year-old-sister. The most intense blowup came because I was given the keys to the car, even though I did not drive and Vivian did. My parents did not want Vivian to drive the car they left in the garage while they were away.

"Give me the keys to the car," Vivian yelled at me one afternoon, shortly after my parents had left to go to the Mayo Clinic for my father's second operation.

"No," I replied, my heart beating so fast I could hardly think.

"I know they are in your room and I am going to get them," she continued. I ran up the stairs to my room and stood firmly in front of my desk. She pushed me away, throwing everything out of the drawers, screaming the whole time. Her frustration increased with every passing moment until she could not take it. She ran down the stairs sobbing, defeated by her younger sister.

I looked out of my bedroom window to see Vivian running back and forth from the driveway to the street in front of our house, appearing to be screaming and crying. Two neighborhood women came out of their houses with open arms, helping to calm her down. Our neighbors in this close-knit community kept watch over us three teenage girls, knowing that my parents were away at the hospital trying to cure my father.

Vivian never tried again to get the car keys.

My parents entrusted me with the keys. I knew I needed to keep them away from my older sister. Playing a trick on her was the only way I could think of to do my duty. The keys were in my dresser drawer: I stood in front of the desk as a decoy so she would think they were in the desk, not the dresser. Devious but effective. She never found them.

Honoring the trust my parents placed in me and standing up to my older sister helped to strengthen my resolve to do the best I could. It helped to prepare me for future life challenges.

Vivian continued to lead a wild teenage life after my father's death, staging drunken parties at our house when my mother was not home, or staying out with boys until the wee hours of the morning, keeping my worrying mother up until she came home.

"The car is missing," I said to my younger sister, Harriet, after we got home from school one day. We knew my mother went to a meeting in one of her friend's car and expected our car to be in the garage. We suspected foul play from our older sister and went to her room to find on her desk a sealed envelope addressed: "Mom."

I said, "If we steam open the envelope and reseal it, no one will know we opened it."

Which is what we did. We hurried down the stairs, turned on the tea kettle, and opened the letter that simply stated, "I have gone away for a few days, don't worry."

Of course we worried.

We showed our mother the letter when she returned home and told her what we had done.

Vivian called us that night from a family friend's house in nearby Elmira. She was ready to come home after receiving good advice from her friend's parents.

After that, Vivian started to get her life together. She went to merchandising school in New York City, worked in a department store in Binghamton, and sold ads for the *Binghamton Press*, the local newspaper.

Anxious to start a fresh life away from her hometown, Vivian took the advice of one of her colleagues at the *Binghamton Press*, who had been stationed at Lowry Air Force Base near Denver. "Denver's a growing western town, with great weather and nice people."

In January 1959, when I was a junior in college, our mother gave Vivian a one-way ticket to Denver and $100. She found a job the first week in the advertising department at Penny's, and met her husband-to-be the next week through a couple she had met on the airplane.

I first felt relieved that Vivian lived out of town, so my mother did not have to worry about her daily. After graduating from college two years later and faced with my own challenge of leaving home, I appreciated and was impressed with the courage it took Vivian to take this step to start a new life—to go to a new town with no job, no money, and no friends or family—and to succeed.

- - - - -

My father's death left a void in me, leading to a lifelong quest to seek out the company of men and boys. In high school I started spending more and more time with boys. Not just in a romantic sense, but for companionship.

To this end I befriended our paperboy, Stuart, who was a couple of years younger, kidding around with him as he delivered our daily newspaper. Stuart brought playfulness to our household as a surrogate brother when male energy was needed. Burdened by the loss of our father, we welcomed the innocence of a fourteen-year-old boy who lived in the present rather than mourned the past.

Perhaps the best contribution to our family was when Stuart came to the house with his friends and we all played cards with my mother. She seemed so happy those evenings.

Stuart and I both had a wild and insensitive side to our teenage antics. Once we played a trick on an old woman who lived alone in a house across the street.

One dark evening we called the Binghamton Police Department. Stuart made the phone call, disguising his voice to sound like what we imagined was a woman over the age of 60. "Help, I am Mrs. Cameron at 20 Vincent Street and there are two strange men walking around the back of the house. Oh dear, one of them just tried to open the back door. Come quick."

After calling the police, we ran up the stairs to the attic of our house, turned out the lights, and watched as one policeman knocked on Mrs. C.'s front door while another walked around the house, looking for the burglars.

"Shhhh," I hissed at Stuart, even though I knew they could not hear us. We giggled together, peeking out through the attic windows like two voyeurs sharing an evil act.

After the police left, we nonchalantly walked down the two flights of stairs to the living room, proud of our cunning. Of course we never told my mother what we had done.

What fun to experience this kind of "guy" thing with my buddy. My girlfriends and I did play tricks on people, but this was different. It seemed less personal, more detached.

I was beginning to appreciate that by hanging out with boys, I did not have to be concerned about hurting someone's feelings, as I did with girls. My interactions with boys were free from emotional involvement. By choosing to be with boys, I could just be myself and not have to satisfy the emotional ups-and-downs of my girlfriends.

This preference for male companionship became more pronounced in college.

In 1956, when I started my studies at Grove City College, about the only hope that a woman could gain a steady job was as a teacher, nurse, secretary, or clerical worker. At Grove City they even had a two-year secretarial major, equivalent to a secretarial school, and a four-year secretarial major, educating young women for executive secretary and administrative assistant positions.[5]

Being a secretary or a nurse was never a consideration. I did not take education courses because I did not want to be a teacher. I chose to be a math major in college because math came easier to me than other subjects, not knowing what kind of job I would be qualified for when I graduated.

I spent a lot of time in college with engineers and the other math majors, mostly boys. Only one girl in my class of 1960 was an engineering student. I liked hanging out with the engineers rather than the fraternity boys because the conversations centered around coursework and other practical matters. There were few pretenses. They were what they were.

I was conflicted about my relationship with my girlfriends. I really disliked when they'd gossip about boys, their teachers, or our other friends. They'd criticize me for something I did not even know I was doing.

"You have been avoiding us," Suzanne said to me one day as we walked to our dormitory. "And you have not been nice to Barbara."

"What are you talking about?" I questioned. I had just made new friends in my sorority and, perhaps, I was not paying as much attention to Barbara as she needed. I was sorry I was hurting Barbara, but did not want to pretend that we were close friends.

I wanted to choose my friends and with whom I would spend time. The boys put less of a demand on me.

I did have to put forth effort to just hang out with the boys, for dormitories in the late '50s were segregated. Boys were not allowed in the girls' dormitories beyond the main lobby. We had curfews. Freshman girls needed to be in the dorms by 8 p.m. during the week, and 10 p.m. on weekends. The older coeds could stay out until 11–12 p.m. on Saturday nights when there were special events.

Outside of classes, the best place to find boys was in the student union. As I found it daunting to walk into the student union alone, I timed my visits to coincide with the engineers' class schedules and sat at the engineers' tables with the boys. I liked hanging out with them rather than the more popular kids in the school, or the jocks.

I spent more and more of my time in college in the company of boys, becoming young men.

- - - - -

As a recent college graduate, I looked forward to expanding my horizons, to seeing the world after touring Europe the previous summer with Pam and Joan. At one point I considered joining a professional synchronized swimming team and traveling the world, following along with a successful synchronized swimming performance in college. Instead I stayed in the United States, satisfying my desire to travel years later, when my professional life took on an international flavor.

It concerned me that my girlfriends from college and high school were following traditional paths, making the choice of getting married or taking jobs they knew would be temporary until they found a husband and had children.

I thought, My girlfriends seem happy they have found a mate, to become wives and mothers. Why am I resisting this role? I want something else.

It wasn't that I did not expect to get married and have children—someday. Just out of college, I wanted to explore my options as a woman in my early 20s.

Fate was with me. Graduating with a Math degree in 1960 at the blossoming of the computer field put me in good stead to find meaningful employment.

Fresh out of college, I was hired as a computer programmer by the General Electric Light Military Division in Schenectady, New York. Having such a job placed me in a unique position among female graduates, allowing me to pursue a professional technical career, working mostly with men, while earning a generous salary "for a girl." I never learned if my annual salary of $5,000 per year compared favorably to the salary of my male colleagues. I just knew I made more than my female friends who worked as teachers, nurses, and secretaries.[6] I loved the security that resulted from being financially independent. I could take care of myself.

I married four years out of college. And my continuing work—to live an independent life, to be a self-determining woman—was about to meet some huge challenges.

It's All in the Name

*A woman has got to be able to say, and not feel guilty:
Who am I, and what do I want out of life? She mustn't feel
selfish and neurotic if she wants goals of her own, outside of
husband and children.*
—Betty Friedan, *The Feminine Mystique*

For the first time someone spoke words I wanted to believe. Reading *The Feminine Mystique* throughout the night in my Manhattan studio apartment in 1963 offered hope. Not the hope of finding a husband and living happily ever after, which was supposed to be every girl's dream in that day. For me, it was the hope that marriage *might* be OK for me. I might be able to marry and still be independent and not lose myself or limit my choices by making my life subordinate to a man's life.

Something inside had been resisting marriage for many years, though having guilt-free sex was appealing. Reading Friedan's words seemed to break down the barrier to marriage. Maybe it was OK for a woman to be a wife and have her own life. I could continue as me and not lose myself in serving his needs and wants.

Betty Friedan recognized that for many women, homemaking was not enough. Some women needed ways to expand their world beyond the conventional housewife role. They wanted to become involved in politics, professional jobs, meaningful volunteer positions. They wanted choices.

A man I was dating at the time asked me to marry him. We dated on-and-off for over four years and had developed a loving and supportive relationship. Dick respected my non-traditional needs

31

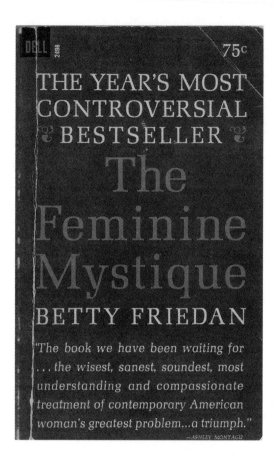

and encouraged me to pursue activities outside of our relationship. He was fun, with his own career ambitions, and knew what he wanted to do with his life. Marrying Dick would provide me with support to proceed with my own career path.

We set the wedding date for six weeks later because I did not want a long engagement period to mull over my decision. Planning a wedding in such a short period of time also provided a reason to have a simple ceremony, asking family and a few close friends. My younger sister served as my only attendant.

Because I was a bride with a deceased father, my uncle came from New Jersey to "give me away." We did have a formal wedding to please my mother—simple but charming, without a huge cost. I wore a plain white dress with a hem just below the knees, with no train or veil that could portray me as a princess. I did not want to be the center of attention.

"I'd like a few tranquilizers," I asked my doctor a few days before the wedding, "To help relieve my anxiety." Taking pills for anything was not my style. Once in a while I would take aspirin for a cold or a hangover—that's all. I felt I needed the tranquilizers to get through the next few days.

I chose to marry a man I loved, to experience the companionship and security that comes from a committed relationship, and to have children. A voice from the back of my head, however, kept whispering, Is that enough? Why do you have the need to take tranquilizers before the wedding? Are you willing to take on the name of, the identity of, Mrs. Richard Mead?

I was also choosing not to be single. I felt great pressure to not-be-single. After all, at 25, I feared others looked at me as if I were an "old maid."

"Why are you not married? You are really good-looking," a friend of my mother inquired. I'd asked myself this same question many times, since all but one of my friends from high school were married and having kids, as were many from college.[7]

A year before, at Pam's wedding, I got drunk at the rehearsal dinner, and because of an incapacitating hangover, I could not attend the reception. As maid-of-honor, I stood at the front of the church with over 200 guests looking on, feeling nauseous. At the end of the service I ran to the back of the church and vomited in the corner of the vestibule.

Being a bridesmaid seven times and never a bride had taken its toll.

- - - - -

The tranquilizers from the doctor didn't help much. The morning of my wedding, I parked my car at the end of Oak Street near my family home, looking at the Susquehanna River, trying to calm myself. I chose that spot because I knew it would be deserted since there were not many homes on the block.

Lorraine as a bridesmaid in friend Linda's wedding

After 15 or 20 minutes I mustered the courage to start the car, accepting the next phase of my life.

- - - - -

Looking back years ago, I recalled an incident on Oak Street that required courage and strength similar to what I needed now to continue with my wedding. I had parked the car near the river where my younger sister, Harriet, almost drowned. Currents of memory pulled me back …

The neighborhood where I grew up in the '40s and '50s was filled with children the same ages as me and my sister. Day after day we roamed the neighborhood playing hide-n-seek, sliding our Flexible Flyers down the Kilmer hill, looking for new adventures.

One winter day, when I was seven and Harriet was five, eight of us kids went to play by the Susquehanna River at the end of Oak Street. We walked along the edge of the river, careful to stay clear of the jagged ice that hugged the banks. Except for Harriet. She kept walking further out onto the ice.

"Stay back, don't go near the edge of the ice," we yelled.

Too late. The ice broke under her weight and she fell into the river. Laden with a heavy snowsuit and boots, her body drifted toward the swift-moving water.

Barbie Dodge and I, with wisdom beyond our age, knew enough to flatten our bodies on the ice and crawl towards my sister before the river washed her downstream. Afraid for our own safety, we inched our way on the solid ice, mindful that once we reached the ragged edges we might also become a victim of the river. With our arms outstretched, we managed to reach my sister and, with herculean strength, pull her, with soaked snowsuit dragged down to her ankles, onto the ice and back to the safety of the bank....

- - - - -

Sitting beside the river the day of the wedding, I tried to muster the same courage I found the day Harriet almost drowned. I knew I needed that kind of strength I'd exerted in helping to save my sister to successfully maneuver as a married woman. I knew there would be challenges, not always appreciating what path they would take.

Returning home from my sojourn on Oak Street, I became embroiled in the festivities surrounding the rituals of a wedding: my sisters, mother, and I dressing in our finest; taking vows in the church where I had spent much of my youth and where my father's funeral took place; and reveling in the good wishes of my friends at the reception.

My joy dissipated when, after the ceremony, my new mother-in-law approached me with this radiant smile and said, "Hello Mrs. Mead."

I cringed, wanting to retreat into a shell. Did being Mrs. Mead mean I had lost my identity? Why was something inside shouting that I was no longer the person I had been? Just because of a name.

I wasn't ready for doubts to surface so early in my marriage.

My poor husband. I cried those first few months, every day, every evening, out of the feeling of loneliness, experiencing a lack of purpose, missing my life in New York City.

We moved to an apartment in Schenectady, New York, because

of my husband's job with General Electric, knowing that he would be transferred in six months to a new position in a suburb of Chicago.

Here I was, having left a secure, challenging job as a computer programmer in a prestigious consulting company in Manhattan, looking for a temporary job in a one-company town in a depressed area. Thankfully, since computer programmers were in demand in 1964, I was hired by the General Electric Research Laboratory for a short-term assignment.

I did what was expected and followed my husband. His employment was the key to a prosperous and happy marriage. The wife's need was secondary, at best.[8]

Now, however, in some relationships, the couple moves in unison, taking into account opportunities available to both parties. Employers call it "the two body problem." That is, in these cases, the employer is expected to provide two acceptable jobs, one for each person in the relationship.[9]

Two months into our marriage, I went to Manhattan with my husband on one of his business trips. We stayed in a hotel in midtown, and then went to dinner with his colleagues.

"The meeting was productive today, don't you think?" my husband said at a dinner meeting with his colleagues. "The client was really rude, but if we encourage his participation in the presentation, he may come around." I first became fascinated with the conversation, proud of my husband's contributions.

I periodically mustered up the courage to get into the conversation. "Our software consulting company had a client with similar problems and here is what we did." I wanted to be part of the group just as I had been while working in Manhattan for four years. No one was interested. They smiled and kept talking about their meeting.

When the conversation became more social I tried again. "When I lived here, we often went to the restaurant down the street— Ethiopian—strange but tasty." Again rebuffed. I stayed quiet for the rest of the night, drinking to escape my despair of not being included or respected—not being recognized as an equal.

I realized then how much my identity was tied to my work. I questioned my belief that a woman could be married and still have goals of her own outside of her husband's life, as I innocently imagined while reading *The Feminist Mystique* only six months before.

The next morning, alone in the hotel room after my husband left to attend his meetings, I cried, and cried, and cried. Desperation over being only Mrs. Richard Mead overcame me. To relieve my hangover I sat in the bathtub, splashing cold water on my face, then my hair. Sticking my head under the cold water, I felt a part of me going down the drain as it flowed over my neck and shoulders. I turned the shower on to warm water to expunge my resentments and to calm my body. Still sitting on the bottom of the bathtub, I grabbed the faucet and hung on to steady myself, to stop the feeling that I could not continue with this life. I knew I did not want to kill myself. I had to find another way to regain the vision of freedom I had as a child.

I chose to keep trying to make the best of my married life. I became more engrossed in my computer-programming job at

General Electric Research Laboratory, even knowing it was a temporary position. I volunteered my time with the Junior League of Schenectady having joined this national young woman's organization my senior year in college because of my mother's social connections in Binghamton.

Four months after that fateful trip to Manhattan, Richard was transferred to Chicago, and—of course, as expected—I followed him to his new job, reticent about

Dick and Lorraine early in their marriage

leaving the Northeast and moving to the Midwest.

Rallying a bit, though, I did find a fun and challenging position as a systems representative with the General Electric Computer Division. In the '60s, General Electric manufactured and sold general-purpose computers, primarily to the banking community. In my new job I provided computer-programming expertise to support the salesmen in securing new customers and in installing their customized applications.

We rented and then bought a house in a trendy suburb. I commuted to work, first in the Loop, then south of the downtown area. Good jobs—I was happy except for the repeated reminders that I was not a whole person.

When we moved to Chicago in 1964, universal credit cards were not in existence. Each retail establishment had their own charge accounting system that required customers to have separate accounts with individual stores.

Being new in town, I had to go to every retailer where we wanted to charge any merchandise.

I decided to apply for some accounts in the name of Lorraine Mead and others in the name of Mrs. Richard Mead, even though I knew the norm was to have credit in your husband's name. By this time in my marriage and career, I'd experienced enough discriminatory practices to have learned much, and I welcomed challenging the norm. I'd been told, "Girl's aren't math majors," having my choices belittled by bosses.

And, after all, in Manhattan, before I was married, I'd had many individual accounts in the name of Miss Lorraine Duvall—at Bloomingdales, Macy's, and Peck & Peck.

I went to the credit section of Sears Roebuck and filled out an application for a charge account in the name of Lorraine Mead.

"An account can only be opened using your husband's name," the clerk at the counter said after reviewing my application. "He is the one who is responsible for paying the bills, not you," she continued.

Shocked that she so blatantly refused to grant me credit, I said,

"But I've received credit from many department stores."

She looked at me, replying, "This is the policy of Sears Roebuck—only your husband's name."

I was done with accommodating ridiculous practices and said, "I will only open an account if it is in my name. I demand a meeting with your supervisor." After making a phone call to set up an appointment, the clerk led me to the other side of counter and took me to a private office in another section of the building. I spoke with the supervisor telling her my story.

"I had many charge accounts when I was single. Now that I am married I want to have a Sears account in my new married name, Lorraine Mead." She approved the charge account in the name of Lorraine Mead only after I told her I would not open an account otherwise.

I tried the same approach with Marshall Fields. That is, after my application for Lorraine Mead was refused by the clerk, I *again* spoke with a supervisor.

The supervisor said, flatly, "We will only open accounts in Marshall Fields in the husband's name."

"But here is all the information about my credit record as Lorraine Duvall in New York City and my proof of current employment," I pleaded. "I will only open an account in the name of Lorraine Mead."

She stood her ground. "No, our policy clearly states that in case of a married couple, an account will only be granted in the *husband's* name."

That was the end of that.

I refused to shop in Marshall Fields until years later, after the women's movement began tackling the issue of discriminatory credit practices. I told my story to the National Organization for Women (NOW), and they in turn relayed the information to Marshall Fields as part of their case for credit equality.

Marshall Fields subsequently opened an account for me in 1972 under the name of Mrs. Lorraine Mead.[10]

The socially acceptable practice of using your husband's name was the norm for formal correspondence and newspaper articles, especially on the society pages. My older sister scolded me for addressing her letters using her name, Mrs. Vivian Reed, rather than Mrs. William Reed.

My nemesis was the custom of the Junior League where your husband's name was required for all correspondence, even signing in for meetings. I remained an active member in Chicago until 1971, when I could no longer keep up the facade by signing into a meeting as *Mrs. Richard Mead.*

- - - - -

My husband and I wanted children and, as planned, after a few years of living in the Chicago suburb, I got pregnant. My employer at the time allowed me to work until the day before delivery of my daughter. I say "allowed me" because many employers forced their pregnant employees to quit after six months or so.[11]

"I'd like to try natural childbirth," I told my doctor at my first appointment after I found out I was pregnant. "I want to be fully there for the birth of my baby—and no anesthesia."

"Forget it," he responded. "Natural childbirth is just hypnosis. It does not work out well for the doctor, the patient, or the baby."

It was time again to push for my choice, for my own reasons and against the expectations of others—in this case the medical community, or at least my doctor.

Undaunted, I continued to research childbirth options to help me make an informed decision. After all, women gave birth to babies for eons without the "help" of modern medicine. Experiencing a miracle as natural as birthing a new human being into this world challenged me. Not only was it better for the mother, but most important, better for the newborn, or so I read in some of the more progressive birthing publications.[12]

I talked to women, asking about their birthing experiences—at work, at social events, and when I spoke with my high school and college friends. Most just looked at me as if I were crazy to not have all the medical help I could get.

Until one day at a cocktail party, a woman I hardly knew gave me my answer.

"I used the Lamaze method. The nurse in my doctor's office gave me some lessons and practices to do at home. But that was back East. I don't know who does it locally in the Chicago area."

"There is a book I suggest," she continued. "It's called *Thank You, Dr. Lamaze.* It's by Marjorie Kamel, a woman who has worked with Lamaze to learn his technique and has even delivered a baby using this method."

I learned a lot about the birthing process from this book. Marjorie Kamel told the story of being trained on the Lamaze method by a nurse and Dr. Lamaze himself, and a subsequent birth while living in Paris.[13]

After returning to New York City, pregnant with another child, she tried to find a doctor willing to work with her, using what she had learned in Paris. She shares her arduous experiences with us in detail, declaring victory after the birth of her daughter:

> All I wanted to do was to have a big lunch and
> call my mother to tell her how splendid life was.

As a result of publishing an article on the Lamaze method for *Harper's Bazaar* magazine, she received many letters from women looking for more information, prompting her to write her book. One letter that really encouraged me to apply the principles she presented in her book was:

> Most American hospitals torture new mothers. They go on the theory that the hospital is there for the nursing staff and doctors ... she is kept waiting ... she is stripped of her possessions. Psychologically she is reduced to a nonentity, a person expected to react like a helpless baby, completely submissive.
>
> Treated this way, like a rubber doll, how can she be expected to participate fully in the birth process?

No wonder Dr. Lamaze made the statement to Marjorie Kamel:

> Many women don't have the self-confidence to
> take kindly to the suggestion that having their
> babies is their responsibility.

I wanted that responsibility. I wanted to have a choice over this natural process. To help gain self-confidence, I took the suggestions from the book to heart. They served as a guide during the last trimester of my pregnancy. Alone in my bedroom, I practiced breathing and releasing exercises.

Day after day I laid on the floor in the bedroom of my suburban home in Hinsdale, Illinois, practicing the exercises suggested in the Kamel book.[14] The Limbering and Posture Exercises in the Appendix were for improving the mother's physical health and for teaching the method of breathing to coincide with the birthing process.

The Appendix also contained preparatory routines for the four stages of delivery. The exercises in muscular control are those I did most. Here's an example:

> Stiffen the right arm and the right leg and raise
> them slowly, letting the left side remain relaxed.
> After twenty seconds, reverse the position: stiffen
> the left arm and the left leg and raise them slowly,
> letting the right side remain relaxed.

The breathing exercises helped me to be aware of my breath and that I could control whether the air I breathed went to my abdomen or chest area. What a learning experience. I began to appreciate the benefit of coordinating my breathing with the tensing and relaxing of my muscles.

I learned later that many of the practices used as an aid to childbirth in the Lamaze method had origins in yoga.[15] For example, the principle of engaging muscles just enough to maintain integrity in the pose without tightening the core is just what is needed during labor, pushing without tensing.

I cringed while reading the beginning section of the Appendix on how to practice, as stated,

> It is advisable to take off your corset and
> brassiere when practicing the exercises …

By 1967 I no longer wore a corset—or "girdle," as we called them. The passage was not that surprising, however, considering the 1951 publishing date of the birthing manual, when women wore girdles regularly.

The Lamaze practice sessions on my bedroom floor were solitary events. At those times I was sad to be alone, needing emotional support and not getting it.

A tenet of the Lamaze method is to have a partner practice with you and to be in the delivery room as your coach. In 1967, very few men took an active part, or interest, in pregnancy issues. At least the men I knew, including my husband. Baby-having was the woman's job. There were no couples' birthing classes in my suburb, and husbands were not allowed in the delivery room.

"You ought to call the doctor," my husband said, as he left for a work appointment on the Saturday morning I went into labor.

The nurse in the doctor's office said—after I told her about the timing between contractions—"You need to come to the hospital. *Right away.*"

The neighbor I called to take me to the hospital did not arrive for what seemed like an eternity. I thought I was going to give birth right there at home. When I did arrive at the hospital, they examined me and wheeled me into the delivery room immediately, saying, "We don't have time to give you any anesthesia so you are on your own."

I was relieved to not have to fight with them. By a sheer accident of timing I was allowed to be an active participant.

The best part: to my benefit, a young doctor, not my regular older doctor, was on call the day of delivery. He and the nurses were familiar with Lamaze techniques and guided me through the delivery process, with enthusiasm, as if we had been practicing together for months.

Mme. Cohen, Marjorie Kamel's nurse in Paris, said to her,

> It is a sporting event. The doctors and nurses are
> the team backing you up.

I felt I was at a football game and we all made up the team. The doctor, nurses, and I cheered along together during the birthing of my daughter.[16]

We named our daughter Jodi Lorraine Mead. I wanted her name to reflect her mother's heritage.[17]

My determination and success in giving birth in a natural way to a healthy daughter left me feeling empowered. Now, however, I needed to mother this child, a task I found to be a daunting challenge.

I was afraid to leave the hospital and take on the responsibility of a newborn baby.

Baby Jodi and her mother

The Anguish of Divorce

You gotta walk that lonesome valley,
You gotta walk it by yourself,
Ain't nobody here can walk it for you,
You gotta walk it by yourself.
> —American traditional gospel folk
> song sung by Pete Seeger

My marriage did not turn out as expected, or as I had hoped. I'd wanted a relationship that was more egalitarian.

At first I found comfort in the companionship of someone I loved and who loved me. We bought a charming Tudor house in a tree-lined suburban neighborhood, made new friends, visited families in Iowa and New York, ate a variety of foods at the numerous restaurants in Chicago, sailed a newly renovated 19-foot sailboat on Lake Michigan, and brought a new life into the world. Both of our careers were going well.

I learned to cook French food, thanks to Julia Child. I loved reading her book *The Art of French Cooking* and watching her shows on television.

But as time went by the marriage started to unravel.

We began sharing less and less of our lives together. Our sex life deteriorated. We argued about money. I felt "less-than"—less-than an equal partner in the marriage, with few opportunities to pursue this independent spirit I longed for before the marriage.

At first I thought the problems with our marriage were no more serious than I saw in other marriages, until my horizons changed. I became more aware of the possibilities for happiness and fulfillment, thanks to my experiences in sessions with the Human Potential group and through reading feminist literature.[18,19]

I don't have to settle into what I consider an unsustainable way of being. There is more out there... and more within myself... that I want to explore, I thought.

To that end, I talked my husband into going to a marriage counselor, actually a minister I met through the Human Potential Movement.

Dick refused to attend after the first session, rationalizing, "This isn't for me, our marriage is OK, it is just an excuse for you to go to a therapist."

I continued to see the minister a few times alone, finding it as hoped, a window into other ways of living. In one session he stood behind me, encouraging me to fall backwards into his arms. It took a number of tries to have faith that he was there and would catch me, that I would not fall to the ground.

I left the session with a glimmer of hope—and with just a little more confidence to step out of a role defined by others.

My husband's job required long hours, exacerbated by the stress of pursuing a master's degree. Commuting to my job in the South Side of Chicago was taking its toll on me, burdened by the primary responsibility of caring for a baby and then a toddler. It became difficult for me to get out of bed in the morning to take my child to school, then me to work. My drinking accelerated.

The sharing of tasks around the house subsided. I said repeatedly to my husband, "At least help with the housework." We had agreed that Saturday mornings would be the time we would clean the house together. That is until my husband decided he had better things to do.

One Saturday morning, soon after our agreement, he announced, "I need to leave to go sailing with my buddies."

Before we were done?

I seethed with frustration, anger, and disappointment.[20]

That morning was a turning point for me. I gave up, not expecting much help from him. From that moment on I began to see clearly where I fit in his scheme of things.

I was becoming what I never wanted to be—a 1970s version of the '50s suburban housewife. I lived as a woman in a man's world. Singing along with Helen Reddy—"I Am Woman"—alone in my suburban home, felt empowering, giving me permission to look beyond the confines of my life.[21] Belting out the self-confirming words of the song reminded me that indeed we women were strong and had the power to forge out on our own—we had choices. I *wanted* to find those choices that would make me feel empowered. I did not have to pretend to be a suburban housewife.

- - - - -

Spending summer days on Lake Michigan, sailing our 19-foot boat, had been an activity we enjoyed together. I say "enjoyed" with trepidation. After we started participating in sailboat races, my husband would yell at me: "Bring the jib in faster, the wind is picking up. Or, "The ropes are getting tangled. I told you to secure them together." Or, *whatever.*

I wanted racing to be fun—he took it as an undertaking to overcome.

Few opportunities presented themselves after our child was born for me to just be on the water, sailing for enjoyment. But my husband went. One 90-degree day, our sailboat needed to be trailered to a marina on the north side of the city for a race. With the baby in the car, I drove to Lake Michigan, where I dropped my husband and the boat off at the marina.

The car overheated in the middle of Chicago as I drove home with a fussy baby. We sat there in the heat of the city for two hours, waiting for help.

I started asking why I let myself be in such compromising situations. I was doing just that, even knowing I did not want to compromise my life.

This was one of the many instances where I played the victim. Perhaps because of a consciousness-raising group I recently joined, I began to examine not only what he did but also how I participated in these realities.[22] With this group of women I received affirmation that I need not sacrifice an autonomous life. I could still be supportive but be independent of his needs. The balancing of equality in our lives challenged me daily.

Why did I *allow* him to drop me and the baby off at the grocery store on his way to a sailing race when I had no other way but to walk over a mile back home with a baby and the groceries?

Why did I *consent* to pick up my husband at O'Hare Airport during a traffic controllers' strike and wait for two hours in the airport with a crying baby? Why did I *not insist* and why did he not offer to take a limousine home?

The state of my health brought changes to our relationship and caused me to examine my role as a mother.

I had a hysterectomy during the years of my brewing unhappiness with our marriage. The results of routine pap smears, the test for cervical cancer, showed abnormal cell growth. In the early '70s, surgical removal of the uterus was about the only way they treated this cancer. I was an at-risk person because my father died of stomach and esophagus cancer and my older sister was being treated for uterine cancer.

I chose to have the operation because of the cancer risk. The doctor showed concern, knowing that at the age of 32, I would not be able to have another child. By then I was questioning my ability to be an effective mother.

My husband said the removal of my uterus changed me. He blamed our divorce on this. If there is any one thing to blame, it is the strength I acquired through the consciousness-raising group I joined—women from my daughter's pre-school. The earlier encounter group I participated in also opened me up to new options for living my life.

Sharing my deepest longings and desires in the consciousness-raising group helped me to realize how my unhappiness was so closely tied to trying to adjust to a predefined role of conventional wife and mother. And to the time-honored role of marriage fidelity. My friends from the consciousness-raising group glorified the new freedom of the '60s to have sexual relations outside of marriage. Many of those married were having casual affairs. Sex with a man other than our husbands was not really wrong, we reasoned—no commitment, just fun.

I had not planned to have an affair—having sex outside of marriage was not really my style. I just wanted something more than what I was getting from my marriage. So I was open when the opportunity presented itself. I became attracted to another man whom I met through my work—Bruce, a professor at Syracuse University.

I fell in love, foolishly thinking I could remain married in the spirit of "open marriage," a fad my husband had encouraged for us based upon the movement popularized by the 1972 book, *Open Marriage: A New Life Style for Couples.* The authors, Nena O'Neill and George O'Neill, believed that self-actualized persons were capable of non-possessive love in their intimate relationships— self-actualized in the sense defined by Dr. Abraham Maslow in his many writings, most notably his book published in 1962, *Toward a Psychology of Being.*

I learned about self-actualization and Maslow's hierarchy of needs from the Human Potential Movement a few years before. Dr. Maslow expounded the belief that the basic human needs of safety and love must be met before one could become self-actualized. Self-actualized people are creative and often unconventional people who have a clear sense of themselves and are not bound by society norms and expectations.

I certainly did not feel self-actualized. In pursuing personal growth and happiness, I looked outside of marriage, outside of society norms. I hadn't meant to develop such a deep feeling for another man. I wasn't even looking for fulfillment in a relationship, or so I thought. My husband and I can stay married and each have outside relationships, I reasoned.

To imagine I could have a "boyfriend" and a husband showed my confusion in my search for meaning in a suburban existence. Handling one intimate relationship was hard enough while still keeping my own sense of self. Two was overwhelming.

Dick thought differently. When I reminded him that an "open

marriage" was his idea, he said, "Yes, but you were not supposed to fall in love. That's unacceptable. It's him or me."

I had to choose, now presented with a clear choice of whether or not to stay in what had become a traditional marriage. In an emotionally fragile state, I agonized over and was unable to understand the ramifications of a divorce. I could not think clearly. Even though I felt trapped in my current situation, I feared leaving the socially acceptable role and following an unknown path.

All I knew was that I was unhappy in my marriage, in love with another man, and needed to pursue my own personal growth free from expectation of others.

I chose to leave.

Dick wanted me to move out of the Chicago area—to move back East, to be out of his life completely. That was doable, even preferable, because I never felt like a Midwesterner. A transfer with my current employer was possible, and Jodi and I could settle into a nice quiet life in upstate New York. We would be near my family and Bruce.

I welcomed the opportunity to return to my roots, to the State of my childhood, to a place I called home.

My guilt over tearing our family apart colored the agreements that followed.

"I am not going to pay for any gouging from divorce lawyers," he stated. I agreed to his choice of a male lawyer—for the both of us—a leader in the men's movement.

Divorces in Illinois in 1973 were only granted "for cause"— causes such as mental and physical cruelty, conviction of a crime, desertion, and adultery. No-fault divorces were being offered in some states where neither party was required to show wrongdoing of the other, but not in Illinois.[23] Adultery could not be included in our proceedings because we had both broken our vows in this way. The "cause" for our divorce was that I had been "guilty of extreme and repeated mental cruelty" to Dick. Neither of us liked putting this in the legal documents, but it was the simplest way to obtain a quick divorce, thereby minimizing cost.

Some issues were easy to resolve—no alimony for either of us and all assets split evenly. Other matters caused much anguish and sadness.

Dick wrote me a note demanding, "Jodi stays with me—no negotiations acceptable."

My heart stopped when I read this. How could he make such a demand? Of course Jodi will come with me—I'm the mother. What does it mean? Neither Jodi nor I can leave Chicago? He will have custody? I won't?

Dick stood his ground, clarifying, "I want custody, Jodi lives with me, you move away—wherever you want to go, just far away."

Knowing joint custody of a child was not an option in Illinois in 1973, I could not fathom not playing a major role in her upbringing.[24] And he demanded the unthinkable—that I not live physically near my daughter.

While choosing to leave my husband was difficult, making the choice to move away from Jodi brought pure agony to my soul. The anguish of separation, of failing this young child, consumed me.

Jodi with her father

My guilt over leaving him kept me from fighting. I loved Dick and did not want to take anything else away from him. I feared an ugly legal battle if I disputed his custody demands.[25] I did have faith—in my mind, at least—that I could make an unconventional arrangement work out in a way that supported the upbringing of my daughter.

My mothering doubts surfaced: I'm not such a good mother anyway; he is a good father; I have friends where the father has custody and that's working out OK; Beth will be there to help.

Beth, Dick's niece, had come to live with us a few years earlier while in high school, because of family problems. Beth became my friend and supporter during this divorce process. In a letter she sent soon after I left, Beth wrote, "I feel as if my best friend is moving away. I really believe now that I am not losing you. I want to help. I want you to know that I love you very much. More than I really realize."

Beth and Jodi

This drive to escape from a narrowly defined female role was becoming more costly than I could have imagined. I was leaving three people—three people *who loved me*. Along with my guilt I felt confusion and fear. Confusion as to why I had this drive to explore non-traditional roles when the world around seemed to accept a life I even questioned from the time I was a very little girl. Life would have been much easier if I'd never felt the need to be independent, never encountered other women who felt the same way I did. But going with the flow of where most of society and most women I knew were headed was definitely dragging me under.

I felt fear in leaving the safety of a known environment, of leaving people I loved, of entering a new stage in my life.

I learned how costly holding onto one's need to be a separate self can be. I could only hope, in the long run, to minimize the harm to my daughter and find ways to continue a supportive and loving relationship.

- - - - -

In the end, Jodi, Dick, and Beth stayed in a Chicago suburb. I moved back East.

My mother and sisters were ready to disown me for letting Dick have custody. My long-time girlfriends from Binghamton tried to dissuade me. During a lunch, with the pretense of a reunion with friends, they spent much of the time presenting all the reasons Jodi should be with me. At one point during the lunch, I provided a reason I had not expressed to anyone before: if he has custody, I know Jodi will still have a mother in her life. If I have custody, I don't know if she will have a father in her life.

I reasoned that even with the miles between us, I would remain committed to mothering my daughter in this unconventional arrangement. What her father would do if he did not have custody I could not predict. So many of the fathers in divorced families I knew did not maintain any meaningful relationship with their children. I wanted her to have two parents. As difficult as it was to make this choice, I hoped it was a decision that would prove beneficial for my daughter.

Dick received sole custody, with free visitation rights granted to me. My legal responsibility included paying for Jodi's education at any private school, including all college expenses. We mostly acted as if we had a joint custody arrangement.

Jodi spent summers and many long vacations with me. Dick and I tried to provide some semblance of family by celebrating Jodi's birthday and other holidays together, often with other family members. Because my employer's home office was in Chicago, I visited every month or two for a week or so, focusing my trips on important events in Jodi's life, such as school and sporting events. A generous friend Barbara made her home our home when I was in town. If Dick wanted to go away, I stayed at their house.

During the first couple of years after the divorce, I kept a log of our times together and a diary of my thoughts, which often contained the question "Why did I not fight for custody?" I looked for advice from other women in my situation, including a friend's friend, Isolina Ricci, who had published a book on shared-custody type arrangements.[26] After meeting Isolina, I wrote her a note thanking her for her insights and shared some of my own. I disclosed my compulsion to record all contacts with Jodi. I did some data analysis of these contacts and attached a summary sheet to my note, with totals of our phone calls during the first five years, by year, and the visits, including the number of days per visit we made to each other's homes. I relayed this information to Isolina to show I was a responsible mother. Most important, I needed to remind myself that my desire to be a responsible mother was forefront in my mind.

Navigating a quality long-distance parenting role without custody was not an easy task. Coming to a resolution when Dick and I had conflicts at times entailed bringing in a third party as a mediator. One instance revolved around Dick remarrying while Jodi was a sophomore in high school. Jodi and the new stepmother did not get along. Jodi also was not doing well in school, and that really got my attention. With much negotiating, Dick agreed to have Jodi come out East to finish her high school education at a prep school in Lake Placid, not far from my home in central New York.

Years later, one of my friends from the lunch in Binghamton said, "You said that Jodi would always have a mother, and she has. I've admired you for that."

That affirmation from a friend who lived a traditional married life meant a lot to me, having lived in limbo between feeling the guilt of self-centeredness and the relief of forgiveness and sacrifice. Not long ago someone asked if I thought that not having custody affected Jodi. I said "Of course." The extent to which I'll never know.

What I do know is that Jodi has turned out to be an accomplished woman professionally and a thoughtful and loving daughter. Her husband and children play a major role in her life. Family is important. She has a need for a solid family life.

- - - - -

The consciousness-raising group I joined when Jodi was in preschool played a major role in supporting me through the divorce process and in charting a new direction in my life.

Part II

Nurturing the Growth

Seeking Solace

There is a sadness in many of your quotations;
as if you didn't know something about life yet,
something you need to know, and can be known.[27]

ALL MOTHERS ARE WELCOME TO
JOIN US FOR A WOMEN'S MEETING
—from a handmade sign posted in the front of
my daughter's Montessori school, Fall 1971

Not sure of what it meant, I took the sign as a daunting challenge. Possibly this announcement was related to the consciousness-raising groups I had read about in the feminist literature. I hoped so.

An attempt to connect with my daughter's Montessori community a few months earlier had been a failure. The director of the school encouraged me to join a bridge group, insisting, "The schooling of your child is a family affair. Even though you work, we'd like you to take an active part in our community."

I tried, feeling trapped as I sat in a crowded room at the school, playing bridge with the mothers of children in the school, most of whom just talked about what suburban housewives talked about rather than paying attention to the cards in their hands. I thought, My attempts at fitting into a conventional housewife and mother roll seem to always fail. Why do I keep trying?

I vowed to not put myself into that kind of situation again. I'd always had difficulties fitting in with the suburban housewife. It wasn't that I didn't like women who made the choice to stay at home, care for a husband, a house, and children. Some were good friends. I just wasn't like them. I know my choice to follow a more independent path seemed foreign to many of them as well. I felt judgment from women and men that I chose to be a working mom, and considered my role as wife and housekeeper secondary to my own needs.

"Why do you allow her to do that when you are home?" Dick's friend Frank asked one evening while visiting, as I walked through the living room with a laundry basket. Dick changed the subject, afraid of my reaction, and remembering Frank's previous remarks on his expectations of the role of wives. Wives were suppose to do the housework during the day so they could serve their husbands' needs at night—and certainly not do laundry.

Frank's attitude was typical of attitudes I encountered in our conservative Chicago suburb. I attempted to broaden peoples' views on options available to women beyond the traditional role of homemaker. The emerging feminist movement of the late '60s addressed the need for changes in society to provide women equality at home and at work.

I made sure people knew my job was my career—that I worked because I wanted to, not because we needed the money. By emphasizing my career to the suburbanites, I was saying that I wanted to be taken seriously, that my choice was different from the choices other wives had made.

I took pride in talking about the newest advances in the computing field and how I relished the challenges I faced every day. Setting the stage this way in a conversation gave me a reason to stay with the husbands and talk about what was happening in the world, rather than with the wives where the conversation revolved around their house and children. I felt out of my element in those conversations. And more than that, I just didn't like chitchat, preferring to talk about computer technology and business issues, which fascinated me.

I remembered with fondness my female colleagues while working in Manhattan. They were different than the Midwestern suburban housewives I encountered at work, at parties, in the

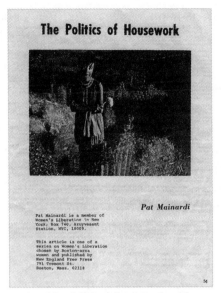

The Politics of Housework

Pat Mainardi

Pat Mainardi is a member of
Women's Liberation in New
York; Box 740, Sruyvesant
Station, NYC, 10009.

This article is one of a
series on Women's Liberation
chosen by Boston-area
women and published by
New England Free Press
791 Tremont St.
Boston, Mass. 02118

A self-published feminist booklet

neighborhood. The women in New York had lives outside of their home. They went to plays and movies with their husbands, their boyfriends and girlfriends, or alone. They talked about technical subjects, philosophy, and politics. They shared their personal frustrations about conflicts between working and raising a family.

- - - - -

In this new group at the Montessori School, I might find women to whom I could relate.

With trepidation I attended the first Women's meeting, not knowing what would transpire. I just knew I needed to find a way to take charge of an unsatisfactory marriage. I was overwhelmed with the challenge of motherhood. I had no one supporting me in this trying time.

The meeting at the school in the fall of 1971 was packed with curious women, about 50 of us sandwiched into a small conference room.

Peggy, the first hippy-looking woman I had ever met, stood up in front of the group, explaining why we were there.

"I called this meeting to share the hopes and dreams I have for my child, Melissa. I wanted to hear from all of you about your ideas as to how we might all contribute as a community to raise independent, free, and loving children. I hope you will be inspired to share your stories."

Here was Peggy, with her long hair and dressed in a bright skirt flowing down to her ankles, talking to us suburban housewives with one thing in common—children in the Montessori school. At that time, the concepts of education put forth by Marie Montessori were controversial and were at odds with traditional educational mores. We were a part of an education revolution.

Peggy did her best in trying to engage us in a group conversation about sisterhood, what it was like to live in the suburbs, our aspirations and problems. Only a few women spoke up. I did not.

Out of the fifty who attended the first meeting, fifteen came back the second time; then ten at the third meeting.

We ten women became the hardcore of a consciousness-raising group. For the first year, we met about once a month in our homes, then two or three times a year for another five years.

"Here are some general guidelines I took from the feminist literature," Peggy offered.[28]

In the early meetings we had each person talk about why we were drawn to joining the group, and tell a little bit of our background.

"I am having a real hard time being a mother," I admitted, relieved that I could finally say this in public. I dared not express my feelings of inadequacy to the other suburban women in our social circle.

"I'm supposed to pick up another child to drive them with my daughter to Montessori every morning. I am always late picking her up because I have such a hard time getting us both ready. And then I am late for work."

"I don't know how to change my behavior," I confessed. "I think this lethargy is a form of depression. Do any of you have this same problem?"

Most of them had problems with their husbands, not with their

Four members of our group—Sally, Peggy, Pat, and Karen

children, although they were sympathetic. A few offered to help by calling me in the morning to get me going.

In some meetings we discussed a specific topic, such as, What are you not doing now that you had expected to do when you were younger. Were you a "nice girl," or what does "nice girl" mean to you. Do you compete more with men or women, and why, etc.

We all shared stories about our husbands and their unwillingness to contribute to the household chores. We laughed at our own feeble attempts during our lives to be self-sufficient and independent girls, then women. We looked for advice when we encountered discrimination in the workplace.

- - - - -

We owned our own bodies by sitting around nude, discussing what we liked and did not like.[29]

One night Peggy gave us an assignment:

"Go home, squat over a hand mirror, and look at your vaginal area. Own your body."

My face turned red as I looked around the room to see how the other women reacted to this suggestion.

Karen looked at me with an awkward smile on her face. The rest seemed unfazed at this request.

It was weird examining myself in the mirror in the privacy of my bedroom at home. To my surprise, it was no big deal. Maybe the others felt that way, since none talked about our assignment at the next meeting.

We retreated somewhat from the recommended agenda suggested by other feminists. We made a notable mistake allowing Karen's husband, at his insistence, to join us for a meeting. He brought a male friend and proceeded to yell at us almost the whole evening: "You are nothing but a bunch of lesbians wanting to blame men for all your problems. Get a life and stop wasting our time."

We conjectured that these men were lashing out at us because we threatened them, their male-dominated society. They saw us not liking men. Therefore we must be lesbians.

At subsequent gatherings I continued to share my personal secrets, hoping that my ability to parent would improve. I shared what often happened after I left work and went to pick up Jodi: "I'd gladly accept my babysitter's invitation (also my friend) when she asked me if I wanted to stay for a drink before taking Jodi home. I did not know what to do with her if her father was not there, since he played with her a lot."

"Many afternoons I would also stop at a store to buy toys so Jodi would have something new to do when we got home. I did not know how to be with my child."

Then, with head bent, I told them when I felt the most shame.

"Many, almost every night, the first thing I do is drink a glass of scotch, often drinking throughout the night. One night, while waiting for her father to come home, Jodi said, 'Don't cry, Mommy, Daddy will be home soon.' "

I marveled at how my four-year-old had such wisdom. I was ashamed that I had burdened this beautiful and innocent creature with my unhappiness.

Confessing my weaknesses helped me to see more clearly how my behavior was making life miserable for myself and others around me. The consciousness-raising group served as group therapy. I found a companionship with women I never knew was possible.

After about three years, four of us had divorced our husbands, to the chagrin of the director of the Montessori School. She told other mothers to stay clear of us and not go in the direction we had followed.

Her fear was valid. A consciousness-raising group did just what the name implied. We recognized the inequality of our roles in the home and society—and did something about it. We confronted our doubts and weaknesses.

"Women of all walks of life and economic circumstances in the cities, in the suburbs, and in rural areas met and shared stories, finding a companionship they never knew was possible. And made changes in their lives," wrote Carol Hanisch.[30]

I made changes in my life that I may not have accomplished without the help of my consciousness-raising group.

Peggy remained single and moved to an apartment in the city.

Karen divorced her husband. Their two children remained with her in their house. She received a handsome settlement agreement.

Pat and her husband separated; they saw no reason to go through a divorce. She continued to work as a therapist and bought a new house for herself and her son.

Linda moved away after her divorce. Their two children remained in the house with her husband.

My husband and I divorced, with him having custody of our daughter.

I fell in love with Bruce and moved back East.

Bruce

I do my thing, and you do your thing.
I am not in this world to live up to your expectations,
and you are not in this world to live up to mine.
You are you, and I am I;
if by chance we find each other, it's beautiful.
If not, it can't be helped.

—Fritz Perls, 1893–1970

After I left Chicago, Bruce and I rented an apartment in Syracuse. I worked part-time for the Chicago-based research institute in Rome, New York, traveling back to Chicago about once a month on business and to spend time with Jodi, staying at a friend's house near her home. I also began a graduate program at the University.

The first year, Bruce wrote me a note on my birthday.

> Welcome to the 35th year of your life. I've been
> part of it for only less than a year but it seems that
> I've known you for years. I wish you love, joy,
> and happiness for the rest of your years and hope
> to be part of them.

We did share joy and happiness together, notwithstanding many trials and tribulations, seemingly different from most couples we knew. We were two independent people, both recently divorced, not ready to commit to a marriage.

Living together lasted for just a year. We found that if we wanted to remain as a couple, our relationship required living apart. Living separately afforded us both the freedom to not be dependent upon each other for our daily existence, while still supporting each other in a committed relationship. We believed the line from the Fritz Perls quote:

You are you, and I am I.

After that first year I rented a house in Rome, and Bruce another apartment in Syracuse. Years later, we each purchased our own homes about a half hour apart, where we commuted back and forth—Bruce in Canastota, New York, and me 30 minutes away in Rome.

With Bruce's son Marshall we formed a family of four, spending much of the summer together and many holidays. Marshall and Jodi, near the same age, developed a brother-sister bond—both children of divorce, each living with the other parent.

Bruce and I traveled together on business since we had mutual professional interests, he as a professor of computer engineering at Syracuse University, and me through my computer programming and systems analysis work. Together we attended computer conferences and meetings around the country and internationally. After all, we first met through a professional colleague, Jerry, who was an engineer with the Air Force Electronics Research lab in Rome.

"I'd like to introduce you to professor Bruce Berra from Syracuse University," Jerry offered, "You two have similar interests because we are also funding some computer database research with the university."

"Yes, sounds good," I replied immediately. Jerry was a sponsor of a significant database contract with my company and I knew to follow his suggestions.

My heart stopped when this tall, handsome man came into the conference room to meet with Jerry and me. His brown leather vest and turtleneck shirt complemented the leisure look of his dark, curly, disheveled hair. I sat tall, wanting to get his attention.

I thought, Get ready, Lorraine, for a drastic change in your life. Here is a man who exudes confidence, appears to know what he

Jodi, Marshall, and Lorraine fooling around at the Erie Canal Park in Syracuse

Bruce joined the party

wants. Remember, you are married.

We clicked. When the three of us drove back to the office after lunch, I turned around, looked at Bruce straight in the eye and said, "Would you like to have dinner with me tonight?"

We did, and as the saying goes, "The rest is history." We ended up in a committed relationship (for 35 years and still counting).

Our relationship had a playful side to it.

The weekend of my 38th birthday, I flew to Chicago to spend the weekend with Jodi. My friends from my consciousness-raising group had organized a birthday party, planning for us all to meet at a restaurant in downtown Chicago, where I was to meet Jodi and my friends and their children.

Airline travel in the late '70s was a pleasant experience. Security procedures were non-existent. Passengers only needed to walk directly from the ticket counter to the gate, showing only their boarding pass. Flights were seldom crowded. Picking up rental cars required only a driver's license.

Names of people who had reserved a car were prominently displayed at the rental car counters on envelopes that contained their rental agreements.

After my flight from Syracuse to Chicago landed at O'Hare Airport, I stopped to pick up my reserved car at the Hertz counter, where I noticed the name Bruce Berra handwritten on one of the envelopes. It took me a moment to register—that might be *my* Bruce, that he was coming to Chicago for my birthday.

"Hi," I whispered to the clerk at the automobile rental counter, smiling all the time. "I think that this Bruce Berra may be my friend and is going to surprise me for my birthday. Would you look to see which one is his scheduled flight?"

The clerk first frowned, then smiled as she opened Bruce's envelope and told me the flight number.

It was the same plane I had just left. Why had I not seen him?

"When he picks up the rental agreement, please do not tell him I know about his renting this car."

The clerk nodded. She was in on the charade.

Instead of going to the shuttle-bus stop to pick up my car, I walked up the stairs to a balcony that overlooked the rental-car counter so I could see him when he picked up his car. Instead of seeing him there, I spotted Bruce hiding near the shuttle-bus stop for the rental car.

"Hey mister," I said in a soft sultry voice as I snuck-up behind him. "Are you looking for a quick pickup?"

We hugged, happy to see each other in this charade. We had a wonderful weekend in Chicago with Jodi and my friends.

I had not seen him on the airplane because he had flown first class, wearing a large brimmed hat.

Thankfully we had these joyful times, for our personalities were often at odds other times. Bruce needed his space more than

Bruce, Lorraine, and Jodi on a Chicago beach

Bruce and Lorraine in Syracuse

I would have liked, mostly revolving around his work. We often argued about how his work took priority over me. I had to learn to accept this or leave.

I learned to accept, and revel in, the freedom to pursue my own path in life and still have the love and support from a caring partner. I began to recognize that the dependence on a man was in direct opposition to my need for independence.

Having Bruce as a partner for so many years made me a stronger person. As a woman it would have been easy, in a way, to accept dependency. Harder, but more fulfilling, to be self-reliant.

Girls & Women

What if we could each gain access to the full range
of human qualities that lie suppressed within us?
—Gloria Steinem

In 1978 (I was 40), a few years after moving to Rome, I joined a second consciousness-raising group—different from the one in suburban Chicago. My participation is the second group in Rome was not so life-changing. After all, the drastic transformation I experienced from being a married wife and mother trying to fit into a suburban role, to living now as a single career woman in a new town with a new boyfriend, far away from my daughter, changed my life forever. I did not expect, or want, another life-transforming experience.

In Rome the group was more analytical, less personal. We seldom talked about husbands—more about the status of women in our town and nationally.

The interactions with the women in both of my consciousness-raising groups helped to clarify how I viewed the roles women and men played in society and in my life.

At a meeting in Rome, a woman named Jean introduced a concept that helped me examine how I viewed gender roles.

"Rather than considering a person as either male or female, reflect on what characteristics make that person a unique individual," Jean suggested.

"Let's do an exercise to help raise our awareness of our biases and how we play into them. First, we'll develop a list of a few universal human characteristics we find desirable in ourselves and others," Jean continued.

We came up with a list of some positive traits.

assertive	analytical	caring	cooperative
courageous	decisive	nurturing	persevering
self-confident	strong	sympathetic	unpretentious

"Then, let's place the words describing these traits along a straight line," Jean continued, "indicating what we perceive generally as male traits on the left and female traits on the right."

The five of us in the group discussed which traits we thought were most traditionally attributed to a male or a female, at times disagreeing where the traits should be placed on the spectrum. Here is a version I liked:

Mostly Male   **Mostly Female**

Assertive   Analytical   Decisive   Cooperative   Nurturing

What an eye-opener for me! I thought, I can just examine what traits I am drawn to in different circumstances along this spectrum of male-female characteristics. Just because I tend to favor men in some situations and women in others, doesn't mean I am being prejudiced.

The word analytical really caught me. I had always wondered why in many circumstances I preferred to work with men. Now I understood that often I just wanted to spend time with someone who could analyze a situation based upon its merits, whether it be personal or business. And men I knew seemed to exhibit this trait rather than women.

Not surprising, having an analytical mind was a necessity in my professional life. I had few female colleagues, though—I worked mostly with men. Seldom in any meeting were there women I would refer to as colleagues.

An exception to that was my three years spent in New York

City. The best manager I ever had was a woman when I worked for the software-consulting firm in Manhattan in 1963.

Most of the women I worked with were ambitious, leading lives that were outside of the norm of my experiences growing up in Binghamton and in college. They were strong women—attending cultural events, possibly alone, taking advanced courses at local colleges after work, and traveling solo internationally.

The challenges with men centered on how some treated me—not cooperating, acting condescendingly to my ideas, not supporting me when I presented different points of view.

If I needed support in a trying situation, I'd most likely go to my women friends. My girlfriends as I grew up through puberty and into young adulthood were instrumental in bringing joy and support to help me become a responsible and fun-loving adult. I have continuing gratitude for the women who were in my conscious-raising groups for their strength and wisdom.

I experienced more nurturing women friends than men friends, but there were times when men provided me with the support and understanding I needed.

An amusing example of how men perceived me in the public arena manifested two or three times a year.

I'd walk up to a clerk, for example, at a checkout counter at a convenience store, and before the person looked at me, they'd say, "May I help you sir?" When they looked up, they'd be all apologetic that they mistook my gender. My presence exuded a male energy more than a female energy.

I'd smile and assure them they were not the first person to do that. Sometimes before they looked, up I'd quietly say, "Ma'am."

Most important, using Jean's suggested method, I learned about myself while contemplating the spectrum of male-female traits. I began to accept that I had many characteristics that society attributed to the male gender, specifically my analytic capabilities and my assertiveness—the assertiveness that developed as I became confident in adulthood when the shyness as a child subsided.

On the other hand, I did not exhibit some traits attributed to the female gender. My nurturing abilities were lacking. I had a hard time cultivating sympathy for situations in which I felt the other person should be stronger.

It is OK if I took a strong stance on getting credit, I said to myself, in defense of contesting the refusal from the clerk at Marshall Fields, an example of how I showed my assertiveness in the past. It is OK if I went to the president of the company to stand up for what I thought was best, I said to myself in defense of treatment from my boss.

At a subsequent meeting, Jean added an additional dimension to the spectrum of male/female traits.

"We have another way of representing human traits. We can take two of the characteristics along the spectrum and make a chart on different axes. It's best to illustrate this," Jean offered.

"Use the 'analytic–nurturing' traits?" I asked, anxious to see how I could apply this method.

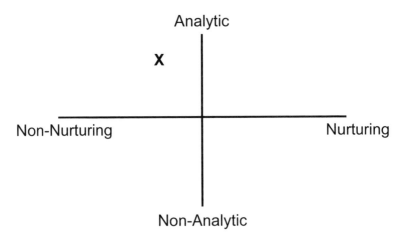

The X represents how I rated myself using this method—placing the X more toward the male-perceived trait of analytic and less indicative of the female-perceived trait of nurturing. Even though this was something I knew about myself, seeing it in graph form helped my analytic mind believe in the reality of the makeup of my personality.

While personally evaluating these traits and accepting accountability, I think of a quote from Gloria Steinem:

> We are so many selves. It's not just the long-ago child within us who needs tenderness and inclusion, but the person we were last year, wanted to be yesterday, tried to become in one job or in one winter, in one love affair or in one house, where even now, we can close our eyes and smell the rooms.
>
> What brings together these ever-shifting selves of infinite reactions and returnings is this: There is always one true inner voice.
>
> Trust it.[31]

In learning to *trust it*, I became more accepting of this lifelong need to direct my own life according to my own personal traits, not just those assigned to me by society.

- - - - -

My professional life presented many challenges in helping to discover, to uncover, to accept and integrate my "so many selves"— my career path that began upon graduating from college and continued for 35 years through my marriage, divorce, mothering my daughter, and my life out East with Bruce.

Part III

Challenging the Norm

Meandering the Maze

Life would be so much easier if we only had the source code.
—Robert Martin

"We need a supervisor for this new software development project; are you interested?"

"No," I replied to requests like these from my managers.

"I'd rather do the technical work."

I did not want the pressure to perform and the responsibility for others. I just wanted to enjoy working with clients, analyzing how a computer system could meet their needs, and helping to program a system they could effectively use.

Being a pioneer in 1960 as a computer programmer meant both women and men were in high demand—gender did not matter. We young women could choose how we wanted to pursue our careers. As a woman in the computer field in the early '60s, I encountered some job discrimination but nothing I could not handle. Single women, as I was then, did not have to contend with the problem of balancing the duties of wife and mother, as some of my colleagues did.

I was treated with respect by my colleagues—many of whom were women—and bosses.

I so enjoyed working. My jobs as computer programmer and systems analyst for large companies and software consulting firms offered me the opportunity to work with a variety of customers with varied needs. Some projects just required simple accounting and banking systems; others required in-depth analysis of areas that pushed the envelope of scientific discovery.

For example, in my first job with General Electric in Schenectady, New York, I helped to program computer systems that studied the engineering alternatives for Project Gemini, the second human spaceflight program of NASA. The objective was to develop space travel techniques for Apollo, the NASA program to land men on the moon.[32]

The computer we programmed was the IBM 650, where punched cards served as the input and output medium. Then we graduated to an IBM 1620 with punched paper tape and a printer. The printer was a luxury—with the 650, the punched cards had to be taken to a separate machine to be printed. Some of the computer programs contained complicated mathematical equations taking, at times, over 24 hours to find a solution. The night watchman monitored the computer to see if the paper in the printer jammed as the computation continued through the night, sometimes all weekend. We'd come to the office Monday mornings, hoping the job had successfully concluded.

After a year, I chose to leave my job with General Electric in Schenectady and move into an apartment with some college friends in Manhattan. I needed more adventure in my personal life and greater challenge professionally.

First I had to find another job.

During the early '60s, overt discrimination was common when looking for employment—there were women's jobs and men's jobs.

Searching for employment in Manhattan in 1961, I responded to the ads listed under Men Wanted where computer programming jobs appeared.[33] The interviews in Manhattan went well since the companies offered employment based on merit. Computer programmers were in demand. Having a mathematics degree suited their needs. Answering a male-help-wanted-ad is how I found my job as a computer programmer for Computer Usage Company, the best job I ever had.

I experienced job discrimination a few years later in the Midwest when I sought employment in Chicago after my husband was transferred.

Upon arriving at Metropolitan Life Insurance Company for a pre-arranged interview appointment, I gave the receptionist at the employment office the name of the person who was to interview me. She stared and said, "You must be mistaken—the jobs for the girls (sic) are in another office, on the right."

Shocked, composing myself, I looked at her calmly explaining, "This is the person I am to see."

She reluctantly allowed me to enter the offices on the left, where the men were interviewed.

It became obvious during the interview that I would not fit into a conservative insurance company atmosphere. In addition to the apparent sexist attitude of the organization, I knew I would find programming insurance applications boring.

I thought, I know some companies offer women similar opportunities as those for men. I will continue to look for something better, like I had in Manhattan.

Indeed, I found a good job with the General Electric Computer Department as a systems representative, supporting new customers. I helped to program applications for organizations within the Chicago area that had purchased GE equipment. Since GE had a computer manufacturing plant in Phoenix, I traveled periodically to Arizona to test the new computers.

One day my manager at GE made a surprise announcement: "At the recent 1964 Miss USA pageant, the winner, Bobbi Johnson, said, 'I want a job as a computer programmer.' I offered her a position as a systems representative. She has accepted and will be starting in a month."

My reaction was mixed. Here was a young woman who used her body as a vehicle to become a celebrity and, at the same time, wanted a position that offered women a decent pathway to a career using their brains. I tried interacting with Bobbi as a programmer colleague, with little success. I did not transcend the prejudice I had against beauty contests.

The actions of my male colleagues may have colored my

difficulty in accepting Bobbi as a colleague. They treated her much differently than me, wanting to help her in any way they could—taking her coat off, interpreting computer manuals, etc.

A news article by Vince Leomard from the *Pittsburgh Press* reveals a similar struggle.[34]

> Here's a girl who could probably make it in show business, so what does she want to be? "I want to go into computer programming," she said. Yes, Bobbi Johnson deals in figures other than anatomical.

The news article revealed how women were viewed in the mid-'60s through his depiction of Miss USA. The reporter goes on to say:

> She's Phi Beta Kappa, National Honor Society, valedictorian in a class of 555, and can type 108 words a minute.

I do not know if he was being solicitous with his typing comment. In any event, he was illustrating that a common evaluation criteria for the value of a woman was how fast she could type.

Bobbi Johnson's employment lasted for six months. She left voluntarily.

- - - - -

As the years went by I started noticing that my male colleagues were receiving promotions, while I was not. Enjoying their work was not their primary evaluation criteria for job satisfaction. The opportunity to move up in the organization, in their career path, motivated them. They looked to the future. I began observing how their approach was different than mine in varying ways.

For example, one of my colleagues, Mark, was upset when our boss went to another company. When I asked him why he was concerned, he answered, "Because I have been nurturing our relationship. Now I have to start all over with a new person." It had never entered my mind that one nurtured a boss in order to get a promotion. I thought all you needed to do was to do a good job. I had so much to learn.

Another colleague, Ken, returned to school in the evening to get a master's degree in computer science to help move himself forward in his career. The challenge of going back to school unnerved me. I had enough challenge just working in a man's world, especially as the years went by and, percentage-wise, as I encountered fewer and fewer women colleagues, discrimination accelerated.

It became more and more apparent that the way women were viewed and treated in the working world dictated and limited the opportunities for us.

Overt sex discrimination in public places presented its own problems, as illustrated by my experiences in public cocktail lounges and bars in Chicago in the mid-'60s.[35]

After work one afternoon, I met a female colleague at a cocktail lounge on the top floor of a 20-story hotel in Oak Brook, Illinois. We ordered drinks at a small table in the lounge area. Shortly after our drinks arrived, the head waitress came to our table with this message: "Women without escorts are not allowed in the lounge from the hours of 5 to 7 p.m."

We arrived before 5 and it was now after 5. I politely said, after a moment's pause, "We will not make a big scene, but want to first finish our drinks."

Then we left, never to return.

Another time I was to meet my new boss at a cocktail lounge in a first-class hotel on Michigan Avenue. He had just flown in from New York City and was already at the bar when I arrived. I sat at a barstool next to him and we started chatting.

Immediately a well-dressed waiter approached, addressing my new boss: "The lady is not allowed at the bar. She will have to leave now."

My boss responded, "She is with me and we plan to stay."

The waiter called to the maitre d' to evict us—so we left.

Encountering this kind of discrimination in public places was certainly embarrassing. More significant, the implication that women were not persons of equal stature with men related subtle messages in the professional arena.

I thought, Why would a company hire or promote me, a woman, over a man if they had to plan around or worry about where I could meet with a client, for example? Why would my boss give me more responsibility when the public message is that I cannot be trusted, that I needed to be defended, to be taken care of by a man?

These questions came to mind, but my consciousness lacked the awareness at this point in my life to understand the full implications of such encounters. I took the attitude, That's just the way it is, even though I knew full well, as a working woman, I did not have the same rights as men.

Something was becoming clearer all the time: These incidents provided an environment where it was difficult to be accepted as a person who could be taken seriously and be provided with any real responsibility. And I was beginning to realize the effect they had on me and my perception of how serious I was in pursuing a career. It was becoming easier to accept the status quo than to try to prove myself. Living the life of a suburban housewife in the late 1960s and pursuing a professional career required a balancing of roles that challenged me as a young woman in my late twenties—primarily alone, with insights from the fledgling women's movement.

My work outside the home lost some of its importance in 1968 when my daughter was born.

For five years I worked part-time, hoping to at least maintain a level of proficiency in my profession. Thanks to my computer background and previous contacts as a software consultant, I was able to obtain a meaningful part-time job with IIT Research Institute (IITRI). Such jobs were scarce for women who wanted to balance their career aspirations with personal responsibilities.[36]

The advancement opportunities for employees who were not full time were almost non-existent—part-timers were considered lesser employees.[37] However, working as a part-time employee in the late '60s was an opportunity to keep myself in the game—I felt I was treading water but at least not sinking, professionally. The rapidly changing computer field made it difficult for anyone, male or female, to keep current with the technology during lapses of employment. I did not want to loose momentum in my computer career.

I wanted to continue to have the daily challenges at work, to have a respite from my responsibilities as a wife and mother.

I also met some interesting people.

In 1969 I shared an office briefly with a recent math graduate of Illinois Institute of Technology, Gloria Karlmark, one of the nine African American students who in 1957 marched into the then segregated Little Rock Central High School, escorted by National Guardsmen. They faced angry protestors on that day in 1957, and harassment from white students the following weeks when they attended classes. After Central High School was closed, Gloria and her family moved to Kansas, where she finished high school.

I spoke with Gloria one day in our office about her experiences during the protests in Little Rock and her subsequent schooling. Unsolicited she said, "I have experienced more discrimination because I am a women than because I am black. More doors are closed and I have less opportunity to pursue my interests."[38]

I expressed surprise. She elaborated, "When I interview for jobs, they ask me about my marital status and when I plan to have children. I can just tell they don't think I'd have a commitment to my job."

I was shocked that discrimination occurred more because she was a woman than because of her race. Her attitude helped open my eyes to see more clearly how discrimination was affecting my career.

In 1970, Gloria and her Swedish husband moved to Sweden, where she was employed as a systems analyst at an IBM research laboratory. She was joining a company with a known policy for treating women fairly.

IBM, the leader in the computer field in the 1960s, had a reputation for affording women opportunities for advancement. In 1964 some IBM divisions started special equal-opportunity programs for women and in 1970 the program went corporate-wide. One of their initiatives included a three-hour course incorporated into their management development programs, designed to raise awareness of the discrimination women encountered.

After graduating from college with a mathematics degree, my first job interview was with IBM for the position of systems representative. They did not offer me a job. A big disappointment. Perhaps I would have received the opportunities and the motivation I needed to succeed earlier in my career if I had started with IBM.

Encouragement for women to take responsibility for their own career path became a rallying cry after new affirmative-action programs were required for government contractors.[39] Barbara Boyle, the woman responsible for designing an IBM program, said,

> In the final analysis, how well a woman does at IBM or any other company depends upon her. If a woman sits back and waits for someone to discover her, the discovery may never take place at all.
>
> She should decide what next two jobs she would like to have within the company and evaluate honestly where she lacks experience for them.[40]

Barbara Boyle continued with her advice to women:

> Women should be prepared to answer questions like, Will you be willing to travel? And will you be willing to move? To get a better job?

Posing this question shows the lack of consideration during these times for the families of working men and women. Good employees were expected to relocate, no matter what the consequences for their families. Primarily the move was prompted by the male's employer. The wives had to leave their jobs, if they had one. The children's school and social life was disrupted.

Married women did not expect their families to follow. That left only single women to decide if they were willing to move for a better job.

I was not open to moving because of a job opportunity. I did move, twice, because of my husband's career.

- - - - -

After my divorce, I asked for and received a transfer from IITRI's headquarters in Chicago to a branch office in Rome, New York—first as a part-time employee while I pursued a master's degree—then full-time. Success in my career became a top priority. Relieved of my wifely duties and not having the primary responsibility for raising my child, I was free to pursue my career with a commitment I had not had when I was younger. Support from my consciousness-raising activities and the woman's movement increased my confidence. While my motivation to move toward a more successful and fulfilling career intensified, I became more aware of and sensitive to barriers placed before me.

I welcomed the opportunity to travel for business. In the early days this included spending a few winter weeks in Florida debugging a system on the client's computers, speaking at a conference in England, and visiting aerospace companies in Southern California. Travel to Asian countries came later.

Discrimination against women in the '60s and '70s, when we were definitely in the minority, showed itself in business travel. Men, and at times women, did not recognize us as individuals worthy of consideration. For example, hotel staff showed little attention to me when I traveled with male colleagues. Even though office-wear for women included skirts and dresses, there were never skirt hangers in business hotels, only in resort hotels. These small instances seem insignificant within themselves, but taken in the aggregate, they tell the story of how society perceived professional women.

I use the word "professional" loosely. One business trip involved flying to Newark airport with two male colleagues to visit a client. The problem started at the airport when our return flight was canceled—the airport was completely closed because of weather.

We could not find any available hotel rooms close to the airport, and ended up south on Route 1 in a fleabag motel that displayed a sign advertising Rooms Available by the Hour. While the desk clerk was checking us in, we asked for three rooms. He winked and said, "We have a great room for three that would be much more fun."

My embarrassment at this overt assumption that I was to provide services for the men stayed with me for years. When my two male colleagues told the story to amuse our fellow workers, I'd laugh on the outside, understanding that each instance of the telling weakened my stature as a woman to be taken seriously.

I became aware of how I might be playing into the subtle, and not-so-subtle, ways my role as a good-looking, recently divorced, single young woman was used to attract clients. At that time I was in a committed relationship with Bruce, but that did not seem to matter to one of my managers.

Once, for instance, my company was hired to develop a computer program to analyze the best methods for determining when a gas-powered engine needed maintenance. I worked closely with my manager (call him Mike) to develop the design for such a system. He always wanted me to travel to the client's (call him Joe) office for design reviews much more often than seemed necessary.

"But we can request Joe's feedback after we submit the design plan. We don't have to go there again," I pleaded.

The travel consisted of a two-hour plane ride and at least one night in a hotel—always lunch with Joe and often dinner with him at an expensive restaurant that Mike, in turn, charged to Joe's contract.

All this socializing began to bother me. When I complained to Mike, he just laughed.

An eye-opening experience occurred at a manufacturing conference in Las Vegas. I went with Mike, planning to meet Joe to attend the technical sessions relating to our project.

Just after we arrived, I ran into Joe in one of the casinos. With a pained look on his face, he led me around the back of a bank of slot machines and whispered, "My wife is here!"

At first I did not know what he meant. Then came the realization that Joe thought we had the kind of a relationship that was to be kept from his wife.

My heart dropped. I felt cheapened.

"Did you promise Joe a sexual encounter with me?" I later asked Mike.

"Oh—what do you mean?" he mumbled. His intentions were very clear to me. Mike never admitted any wrongdoing—perhaps he felt it was not wrong. Perhaps he felt it was OK that women be used as favors for men.

From then on I became more aware of my behavior and how my actions might be taken as a sexual invitation.

This awareness of the sexual tension in the workplace was just one aspect of how I changed my approach to my job.

It wasn't until my mid-thirties, after my divorce, that I became mature enough to accept the greater challenge of moving into a management role. I'd begun to practice yoga and meditation, sharpening my consciousness. These esoteric practices helped me to become aware of the importance of doing a good job to its fullest, no matter what the task.

I realized that I often knew more than my managers, all men, and thought, I have the confidence to leave the comfort of the computer programmer role and expand my sphere of influence.

My self-esteem increased—I had much to offer. I was promoted to manager.

I enjoyed the challenge of interacting with clients and organizing projects to fit the capabilities and interests of the software engineers and support staff. My ability to obtain new business resulted in hiring new employees. I was given the responsibility of managing an additional department, further increasing my sphere of influence.

Then came another realization.

As I became more assertive in moving ahead in the organization and my responsibilities increased, I noticed that recognition and promotions were slower for me than my male colleagues.

Manager of Operations or Branch Manager or Assistant Research Director were titles they offered me when others, all

Lorraine's first employees as a manager

men, who had the same responsibility, had the title of Director of Research. Over 100 people worked for me. I had a successful track record in bringing in new clients.

After insisting on a title commensurate with my position and responsibilities, I was promoted to Director of Research. There was no way of knowing, however, if my pay was equal to men holding the same position.[41]

Though many women in the computer field, including me, had been provided professional career paths not available in other lines of work, we became concerned about what appeared to be different monetary treatment between men and women, along with other discriminatory practices.

The Equal Rights Amendment (ERA) addressed our need for equal opportunity in our jobs and heightened our awareness for action.[42] Our advocacy came to a head at a conference I attended in 1978, held in Atlanta, Georgia by the Association for Computing Machinery (ACM), a leading national and international professional organization.

I was a part of a group of women attending the conference who drafted a proposal to the Board of Directors requesting that, "any subsequent meetings not be held in states that had not ratified the ERA," Georgia being one of those states. Our proposal was rejected by the board, stating that the ACM did not take any stance on political issues.

We believed that an economic boycott of those states that had not ratified the ERA was making a difference.[43]

While we were at the conference, ten of us, all women, met to explore what actions we could take as computer professionals. One was to form the Association for Women in Computing (AWC).[44] I became the first president. Our purpose was to advocate for common concerns among workers in our field, and act much like a professional version of a consciousness-raising group.

My involvement in such job-related organizations gave me confidence to counteract the conflicts that were brewing with my boss (call him Jim).

In 1981 when I was promoted to Director of Research, I managed a group in Rome, New York, reporting to a vice president in Chicago. In a subsequent reorganization I had a new boss, a newly appointed vice president based in the suburbs of Maryland. With this promotion, he became responsible for a small branch office in Maryland along with our branch office in Rome.

My voice shook as I announced this reorganization to the employees in Rome, disappointed that I had not been promoted to vice president.

Was I being passed over because I was a woman? I asked myself. What in my performance had been lacking? We had doubled our annual revenues under my leadership. Wasn't that enough?

These nagging questions stayed with me. I did, however, like Jim and hoped that everything would be OK, although he had shown a tendency to treat women with deference, as perhaps the "weaker sex," rather than respecting us equally for our ideas and problem-solving capabilities, and rewarding us accordingly.

For example, Jim organized a party to thank a group of us who had worked hard on a large proposal, working nights and weekends to produce a quality product.

He presented each of us with a memento of thanks—the men a commemorative wooden plaque with words of praise for their contributions—for me and Pat, the wife of one of the men, a bouquet of flowers.

A bouquet of flowers for the women!

Politeness ruled over my first instinct to throw the flowers back in his face. Instead I complained to those who might have an understanding, asking, "Jim's actions were not appropriate and were demeaning. Doesn't he see that?" A few seemed to understand that the different treatment of the men and women showed a sexist attitude; most did not. I was disappointed that more of my colleagues lacked the awareness I had gained in my consciousness-raising groups and through the women's movement.

This was a "click" moment—a moment of recognition and a confirmation that there existed little sensitivity in my working environment for discerning discriminatory practices. When Jim gave women flowers instead of a commemorative plaque, he revealed his "thanks" as a permanent gesture to the men, as a temporary gesture to the women.

Jim began showing preference for the group in Maryland by recommending larger raises for the Maryland employees and investing in their projects, to the exclusion of ours. Jim's preferential treatment increased after my group in Rome won a contract to develop a plan for a statewide utility company to apply artificial intelligence techniques to the operation of their utility.[45] This new venture illustrated the dynamics of our group that, in my opinion, was not a trait the Maryland group exhibited.

In the midst of this brewing rivalry, my company sent me to Cornell University for their five-week Executive Development Program. I felt good about this opportunity since it meant they had faith in my ability to continue the rise up the organization.

The management course increased my confidence in my ability to lobby for more cooperation from Jim and upper management.

Lorraine's employees outside the Rome office in 1984

I was not successful.

About a year later Jim called on the phone, announcing, "I have transferred the Ada contract to the Maryland office."[46]

I could not believe it. This major program directed out of our office in Rome was a lucrative financial resource. Several years earlier, despite a low probability of winning, we had secured that contract, demonstrating our ability to attract new business in a growing computer initiative.

I hung up the phone, wanting to scream. Instead I talked with a colleague, saying, "I'm ready to quit or am willing to do something that would cause me to be fired." I was not thinking clearly. He calmed me down by saying, "You are very happy with your lifestyle. Do you want to do something that would change that—what are your goals?"

I left the office for the afternoon and walked in the woods, contemplating my options. I could not see my way clear out of this conflict.

My frustration intensified as Jim took more and more liberties in manipulating the financial data.

"But Jim, the way the financials are reported does not give credit where credit is due— namely Rome," I pleaded.

He'd reply, "That's OK. We need to do it for ...." and he'd give some excuse.

Morale was low in Rome. My team saw what was happening. My energy was drained. I stopped looking for new business, concentrating on holding onto what we had.

I knew I needed to do something to change the tide. But what? I lacked any role models ... no one I could talk with to discuss the best way to precede. Thankfully I had my yogic practices to help find a way out of the situation. Passively accepting the status quo did not fit into my newfound confidence. I chose to take a bold approach—I went to the company president.

When I called the president's secretary in Chicago to make an appointment, I asked her not to tell people I was coming to town. Then I had my secretary make plane reservations for Chicago, also asking her to keep this trip to herself.

When I was seated in the president's office, I braced myself and went for it.

"Here is my plan," I told the president. "Since Jim is a wonderful promoter and makes a good impression with clients, but is not such a great administrator, appoint him to be in charge of a new division responsible for client relations."

The president was complimentary of my past performance, but listened to my concerns noncommittally.

Seeing that this was likely to go nowhere, I went to the next level.

"I can't work for Jim anymore," I announced stating the reasons why.

I left the meeting understanding that the President wanted to meet with Jim and me to discuss alternatives.

"Jim wants you to call him," my secretary said when I returned the next day. "Right away."

"What do you think you are doing!" he yelled on the phone. "I want you to come to Maryland immediately."

Undaunted, I flew from the Syracuse airport (the nearest airport from my home in Rome) to the Baltimore/Washington Airport the next day, not too worried, since I thought we could work things out.

Jim met me at the airport, and instead of going to the branch office, he took me to the basement of his home, his home office. He proceeded to yell at me for two hours. I sat there stunned as he told me in myriad ways what a bad job I was doing and how I did not understand the business.

I was trapped in the four walls of the basement with no escape, certain that nothing I could say would change anything.

I could just run up the stairs and walk out the door, I thought. Then what would I do? Here I was in a suburban neighborhood in Maryland with no means of transporting myself away from this hellhole.

We went to lunch and I sat there unable to eat, intimidated to the point of helplessness. I could not think of what to order. I questioned whether I would even be able to get back to my home in Rome; I was that shaken by this ambush.

Jim took me to the airport, instructing me to come to Washington the next week to meet with him and the president.

- - - - -

I met Jodi for dinner that night in Syracuse, trying not to show my distress. I thought, Jodi has her own ordeals as a sophomore at Syracuse University. She doesn't need to be burdened by the problems of her mother. As we ate dinner together, I realized that the primary reason I loathed telling her about my humiliating experience in Washington was because I was ashamed—ashamed I was not tougher, not strong enough to carry my own weight in the business world. I did not want my daughter to see her mother in a weakened state.

The next morning my confidence returned, hoping the president would find a solution to our conflict. After all, at our previous meeting in Chicago he showed support for me and my accomplishments.

The scene in the hotel suite in Washington the following week, however, told a different story.

When I arrived, Jim and the president had seated themselves at one end of a large conference table.

"Sit down over there," Jim said, with a stern voice, pointing to a lone chair at the other end of the table.

The scene was out of a scary movie. The two devils merged as one at the end of an infinitely large, brightly polished mahogany table, sending daggers to the innocent girl across the way. The girl who had no defenses.

I did sit there. Wounded. Once again I was the victim, with no strategy, no protection from the onslaught of negativity I was to receive.[47]

For the next hour, Jim presented his evaluation in the form of a formal performance review—a negative review one would give to lay the groundwork for firing someone. He had to balance out the glowing review he'd given me six months earlier.

I knew he was grandstanding for the president. He was not going to let me get away with circumventing his authority.

The negativity spewing from his mouth was easier to take than the disastrous scene in the basement office in suburban Maryland. I did not feel as intimidated with the president at the other end of the table, although he just observed and did not say anything.

At least we were not alone and I had an escape if I wanted one. I could walk out of the hotel and grab a cab to the airport, I thought.

And I was correct that I was being shown the backdoor.

After it was announced that I was leaving the organization, Jim spread the rumor that I planned to charge the company with sex discrimination. At the exit interview with the president I said, "That's not my style."

He sympathized, offering his opinion. "I understand why you were not happy with how Jim treated your operation in Rome."

Then why did he never come to our defense? Was he also

intimidated?

Later I did go to a feminist lawyer, asking if I had a case, specifically how I was harassed in the basement office in suburban Maryland. She said, "No. He was just a jerk, a bully." Yes, that is what Jim was—just a bully.

After I left, Jim reminded the employees, primarily the managers, of his philosophy: "You can get on the train, or you can get off the train. But if you get in front of the train, I'll run you over." The bully had run me over.

Jim promoted a woman from the Maryland office to take my position. She only lasted for six months. It was an example of a woman being placed in a job just because she was a woman, not because she was qualified. When it does not work out, we women get a bad name.

"Do you think I could have been a vice president?" I asked a previous boss, who was a VP. "Sure," he said. "You have what it takes—you showed you can successfully grow and manage the business."

I needed confirmation that a path to more responsible positions was available to me within the organization. Making the decision to approach the president may have been an unwise choice. It was, however, the choice I made. This choice opened up new possibilities, more than I could have imagined.

Even though my ego was crushed, I welcomed the opportunity to chart a new direction. I was comfortable financially. My only fiscal responsibilities were to myself, and my daughter's college expenses with, thankfully, only two years remaining.

- - - - -

While building a career, I was also on a spiritual journey that provided me with strength and support, both personally and professionally. It began shortly after the divorce, as I entered a new phase of my life.

Part IV

Waking Up the Self

Another New Beginning

When you do things from your soul,
You feel a river moving in you, a joy.
— Rumi

The anguish of my divorce in 1973 and the absence of my daughter in my daily life weighed heavily on me. Bruce and I argued a lot of the time. I had difficulties handling the stressful situations in my job. I began a master's degree program at Syracuse University, more challenging than anticipated.

I knew I needed to find a way to come into harmony with my new life at the age of 36.

So I began a search from my new home in Rome, New York, where I was living after the divorce and the move East.

The Rome Y offered a number of different activities that seemed interesting.

I first tried a belly-dancing class and soon found that was not my thing.

"Let's try the yoga class instead," I said to a fellow belly dancer who also had a hard time moving her hips to the Arabic music.

It did seem strange that in 1976, a yoga class was offered in such a conservative place as Rome. This small city had an air force base and a very Roman Catholic population. I knew yoga was emerging in more populated areas as, I surmised, an integral part of the New Age movement, but here it seemed unlikely to take root.

As I stepped on the yoga mat my first day in the class, I didn't know how this ancient practice would chart a new direction for the remainder of my life.

Clare, the yoga teacher, invited those interested to stay for meditation after the hatha yoga session that day. I stuck around, curious. Four of us sat cross-legged on our yoga mats in a circle in a dark room at the Rome Y. Clare lit a candle in the center of the room, guiding us into meditation. She encouraged us to first look at the light, then to close our eyes and watch our thoughts.

Immediately after I closed my eyes, I felt this shot of energy going up my spine and out the top of my head, as if a vacuum cleaner was sucking up the dirt.

What is happening to me? I thought. How can I stop this energy from blowing up my brain?

Conversely, my body became more relaxed once I stopped judging the experience. My head did not blow off. I was still sitting on the floor with the same people I was sitting with five minutes earlier. Or seconds earlier, for the time had gone so fast.

I felt both fear and fascination. Fear that I did not know where such a mystical experience would lead. Fascination that I may have more such experiences that would help me to feel lighter, less burdened.

I shared my experience with Clare, asking, "What does it mean? It scares me."

Clare seemed surprised such a thing happened to her student in the first meditation session.

She asked her teacher and later told me, "Your experience was quite significant in the spiritual sense. You had what's called a Kundalini awakening. The spiritual energy, the Shakti, ascending up your spine is the beginning of an opening to your Greater Self."

Confused but intrigued by my experience and her explanation, I began exploring meditation further. I joined with Clare and a group (from the Central New York area) involved in chanting and meditation, led by Ram Butler. Ram wrote a correspondence course on yoga philosophy and held workshops in which he taught and led chanting and meditation sessions.

Ram, a tall handsome man in his early forties, had started meditating as a teenager, and readily shared his understanding of

Eastern spiritual philosophy.

Ram believed that most of us only glimpse sublime happiness and joy because we are so involved in our daily lives. We don't even notice an inner bliss as we search for happiness where it is not. The reason we practice spirituality is to experience this inner bliss.

I dared not think that I could obtain this inner bliss. A journey to discovery was enough—reading the lessons from Ram's correspondence course, attending the workshops, and chanting in the Sanskrit language with the group of spiritual seekers.

"Thank you for introducing me to a way I can get in touch with a part of me I never knew existed," I said to Clare after one of the chanting workshops. "This is a new beginning for me."

Most supportive of this search for a new beginning was living in Rome. It brought me in touch with people who were searching for what Ram called this inner bliss.

I met wonderful people also new to and intrigued by the enlightened teachings based upon yoga philosophy and spiritual texts.[48] We chanted and meditated together in peoples' living rooms and basement rec rooms, in community centers, rustic barns— wherever we found accepting places to gather. Most sessions were held within driving distance from Rome; some were in Florida where Ram lived for a short period of time.

A few of us met weekly in our homes to chant and meditate. Clare played the guitar or the harmonium to help us keep in tune with the melody of the chant. I loved singing "Govinda Jaya Jaya."

Singing the Sanskrit words representing the divine power of the universe brought me in touch with a peace and contentment within myself that would last for days. I could take on any challenge. Even the challenge of playing a musical instrument.

I learned how to play the cymbals to set the rhythm for the harmonium, and to help us stay with a beat as the pace of our chanting increased during a session. We lit candles and burned incense, usually one named sandlewood because it gave off a scent of nature, of the woods.

My diet and way of eating changed.

An altar used during our chanting sessions

I learned about a macrobiotic diet from my newfound friends. Changing my diet into something more healthy intrigued me. I could take care of my physical body as well as enhance my spiritual being.

I made an appointment with a macrobiotics consultant who provided advice on how to eat a healthy, balanced diet, centered on the use of grains and fresh local vegetables.

"How often do you eat meat?" the consultant asked. I'd been cutting back on meat, especially beef, and replied, "Once or twice a day," proud of myself that I seldom ate meat at breakfast and sometimes not at lunch.

She looked down, averting her eyes from mine, and spoke slowly and quietly. "Do you know that we suggest eating very little meat and only if raised in a natural environment? Fish or chicken perhaps once or twice a week."

I felt dumb not knowing the basics of this new way of eating. I felt even worse when she asked, "Do you take drugs, smoke cigarettes, or drink any alcoholic beverages?" I said no to the drugs and yes to the cigarettes and alcohol. She gave me a dissertation on the harmful effects of cigarette smoking.

I stopped smoking cigarettes three years later.

When I admitted I drank one or two or three scotch cocktails a day, actually a perfect-Rob-Roy-on-the-rocks-with-a-twist, with the addition of wine during dinner, she gave me this bizarre recommendation: "If you insist on drinking alcoholic beverages, I suggest you consider drinking Japanese sake (a rice wine), or Rolling Rock Beer. Both of them contain very little, if any, harmful chemicals." I was happy to hear this suggestion—I liked sake.

I began drinking only sake, with an occasional glass of wine when sake was not available. I stopped drinking alcohol fifteen years later, in 1995.

I bought the book *Macrobiotic Cooking for Everyone* by Edward and Wendy Esko to help understand the fundamental principles of macrobiotics, how to arrange my kitchen to accommodate the changes in my cooking, and to get instructions on meal preparation and cooking. I asked for suggestions from my friends on ways they had incorporated this style of eating into their daily lives, and began including grains and vegetables as a mainstay of my diet, enhanced with some fish and chicken.

"What do I do with the beans in this bin?" I asked the clerk the first time I shopped at a health-food store, looking for foods to suit my newfound diet. I felt foolish as everyone else in the store seemed so self-assured, easily maneuvering their way around bins of beans, seeds, nuts, and fresh herbs.

This new way of eating fit into the vegetarian diet practiced by most of the participants in the yoga retreats.

At the workshops and gatherings we laughed, cried, and shared our spiritual experiences, asking for guidance on how we could apply the teachings to our daily lives. Our laughter usually came when we saw how absurd our life manifested itself, sharing common experiences. Someone in the class would often tell their story of being pulled quickly off-center.

One day I shared an experience I'd had in the car, a common occurrence others have encountered.

> The other day I was feeling really peaceful, riding to work after having a good morning meditation. Just as I was entering an intersection, the guy who had been behind me pulled alongside, and then in front, cutting me off.
> I swore at him, honking my horn loudly. Any semblance of civility left me.

We shared experiences like that to put us in tune with our absurd lives, and to show how our practices needed to be strengthened. The challenge was to stay centered as our daily challenges presented themselves.

During a neighborhood softball game—I coached one of the teams—an instance occurred that left me thinking how my meditation helped.

I had volunteered to coach when Jodi was in Rome for the summer of 1980, since the team of 12–14 year-old girls needed a coach or they could not join the league. I did so reluctantly, unfamiliar with the rules of the game.

The girls often taught me about the game during practice sessions. One day I yelled, "Jane, move over to middle field."

The girls laughed, yelling back, "It's called *center*field." Jodi was so embarrassed at her mother's lack of knowledge.

It started to rain heavily during one of our softball games. After the fourth inning, the coach of the opposing team asked if we should postpone the game. I said, "Sure, we should get the girls into a dry place."

The coach turned to his team announcing, "Yay! We won another one!"

"What?" I yelled. "We will play the game over at another time."

He informed me that the rules stated, "If a game is called after the fourth inning, the team that is ahead is considered the winner of the game."

I was furious. Angry at myself for not knowing the rules. Angry at the other coach for not being straight with me. I, just for a moment, started yelling uncontrollably, repeating over and over again, "This is not fair. This is not fair ..."

My voice became shrill, different from my normally low monotone.

Then suddenly I remembered—remembered that what was happening on the outside need not affect my center being. Thanks to my esoteric practices, I came back to my senses and began reasoning with the other coach.

Becoming aware of how my spiritual practices supported my daily life, I increased the time spent meditating, chanting, and contemplating spiritual texts.

Tears often came to my eyes and my throat tightened when I sang chants in the Sanskrit language.[49] One of my favorites, "*Narayana*," made me feel protected as, in our homes in Rome or at retreats, I repeated each verse of the chant with a group of meditators, at times for as many as 20 to 30 minutes.[50]

The tears came from an emotional release opened up through chanting. Often during and after a long chanting session, I'd think, I can transcend my problems at work. I can move forward, or around it, rather than have it stop me.

I marveled when I saw a car bumper sticker that said, "I'd rather be chanting." I wanted that bumper sticker to help announce, "See how my life has changed. I am no longer a suburban housewife trying to fit in with the Junior Leaguers. I am following my heart."

I did, however, have doubts about following a mystical discipline that was outside societal norms. I wanted the discernment to understand the joy and freedom that this yoga brought to my daily life, the release that came from feeling a union with something greater than myself.

Holding on to my need to be an independent woman seemed in conflict with releasing to a higher self. I feared a dependence upon a spiritual teacher, and practices that made me vulnerable. I wanted to be in control of my actions.

"I don't like you hanging around with those people," my mother said, with an edginess to her voice. "They will probably take all your money."

"I'm careful Mom," I replied. "You met some of my friends. Don't you think they are nice and level-headed?" She'd look away, mumbling something about not trusting my teachers.

The '70s was a time of great change in our country with traditional social mores in flux. Sexual freedom became prominently accepted in the media. War and civil rights protests were rampant. Two of my mother's daughters were divorced. Her grandchildren were not being raised under her philosophy of "Children are to be seen and not heard."

And her most responsible daughter was taking-up with a strange Eastern philosophy.

Bruce on the other hand seemed happy with my meditation practices. "We get along better after you have spent time with your yoga buddies," Bruce said when I'd return from a retreat—Yoga Camp, as he called them.

He was right. I was easier to get along with after I spent time chanting and meditating. Studying the ancient yoga philosophy helped me to better understand when I was acting under pride, or letting my ego dictate my actions. By clearing my mind of negative thoughts, I was able to see how I could make a situation better, rather than worse. I handled stress at work with greater clarity.

I did, however, proceed with caution as I pursued this esoteric path, not wanting to lose my sense of reasoning and my moral compass. I experienced many doubts about following an unproven (at least to me) mystical spiritual path.

During the first years when I was studying with Ram, a strange thing happened that helped me look inside myself and discern how I could learn from what was happening in the world.

While changing planes at the Chicago airport on my way home from a retreat with Ram in Florida, I became frightened as I watched the television in the airport lounge. The killings and suicides in Jonestown were being reported.[51] The TV commentators gave the account: "Hundreds of people were found dead in Guyana at the site of a commune lead by James Jones, this charismatic leader who had just moved 'his people' from San Francisco to escape so-called persecution."

I did not want to be a part of a cult that brainwashed people. I continually checked myself by questioning how my life was being affected by following this yoga path.

Questions I contemplated were these:

> Am I having fun?
> Do I have enough discrimination entering this unknown territory?
> Will I be a better, happier person because of following this path?
> Am I opening myself up enough to the benefits the ancient yogic teachings can provide?

In fact, I *was* having fun, more than I'd had since I was a kid. And I began trusting my ability of discernment to distinguish among the true teachings and those that did not make sense in my life. Chanting and meditation brought me the peace and strength to find new ways to improve my relationships with Bruce and my daughter Jodi, and to tackle challenges in my job.

My daily experiences, and most important, how I viewed my life, began changing for the better. I was happier than I had been in years. Hanging out with a community of seekers provided support not experienced before in my life.

Physical manifestations of energy moving through my body continued after that first Kundalini experience with Clare. I discovered this was good. Old patterns and past impressions were being released.[52] I was beginning to understand the acceptance of change; that the only constant in life *was* change; that releasing, letting go, was paramount to finding peace in this world—to finding that mystical "inner bliss."

I took these questions into account when Ram talked about his meditation teacher, Baba Muktananda. Baba's home was in

Ganespuri, India. Ram encouraged us to go meet Baba when he was in the Ashram in Oakland, California, on his third tour of the United States.

My curiosity got the best of me, and I flew to California in March 1979 to attend a meditation retreat so I could meet Baba. A group of people who met Baba on his previous tours of the United States purchased and refurbished an old hotel in downtown Oakland to serve as a meeting place for yoga practices for themselves and visitors. They served meals in the dining room, and chanted and meditated in a large hall (capacity about 250) outfitted with a few chairs in the back of the room, and cushions in the remainder of the hall for people to sit on the floor.

The night before the retreat—Friday night—Baba sat on raised cushions and greeted all who were interested in meeting him. I was reticent at first—then decided to be brave and walked to the front of the hall to be introduced to Baba.

When our eyes met, I felt he looked at me as if to ask, "What are you doing here?" which was the question I was asking myself.

I stayed for the remainder of the weekend, curious as to what would transpire and how I'd react to the words and actions of Baba and the other attendees. I did know a few people from the Rome area, and some I'd met while attending Ram's workshops. Ram was also there with his wife.

I asked Bindu, a friend from Rome who had been at the Ashram in Oakland for a week, "I'm so happy to see you. How has it been going for you?"

"Pretty intense," she replied. "Many of my old issues are emerging that I need to deal with. Hopefully at the retreat this weekend I will get some answers."

I felt relief in seeing a yoga buddy from home and to hear she survived a week in the Ashram. I had flown to Oakland with great trepidation, sensing that meeting Baba and attending a retreat could cause a great shift in my spiritual practices.

My previous spiritual endeavors equated to putting my toes into a cool mountain stream. Attending a retreat with Baba Muktananda was jumping into the deep ocean. I did not know what the weekend would bring.

Saturday and Sunday, Baba gave two talks each day through an interpreter, since he only spoke Hindi. He spoke of the ancient philosophy of Kashmir Shaivism, some of which Ram taught. Shaivism is a particular approach or aspect of Hinduism that focuses on the Shiva, considered to be the Supreme God within us and in all things.[53]

At the retreat, we chanted and meditated as a group. I experienced the same kind of energy while in Ram's retreats, heightened by the presence of Baba and the 250 other students.

As was the practice in these retreats, Baba walked around the hall, touching people lightly on the top of the head. This gesture constituted the transmission of spiritual energy from the teacher to the student, a form of initiation to open up the student to the possibility of a spiritual awakening.[54]

When Baba touched my forehead I experienced a life-transforming meditation. The journal entry I wrote after that weekend relayed this experience:

> When Baba walked around the room and stood near me, I said to myself, OK Baba, let's see what you can do.
>
> After he touched me on the top of my head and forehead, a solid mass of blue light appeared in my vision; white specks permeated the entire spectrum.
>
> All this was behind a window frame, with me looking through the frame into the blue light. I knew that if I jumped out of the window, it was the end of Lorraine as I knew her—the end of the limited self.

In awe of this experience, I asked a number of people in the Oakland Ashram that weekend what it meant, trying to make some sense of my fear and confusion. Experienced practitioners, people in the know including swamis, said, "Meditate on what it means to you. Baba sent you a message."[55]

Reliving and meditating on this experience became a central part of my yoga practices. I learned to be careful in sharing my spiritual path with my worldly friends and colleagues, musing on what the poet-saint Tukaram Maharaj said:

> When a yogi describes his experience of inner
> bliss, people are awestruck and wonder if this
> strange experience could be true.

Some of my friends and family started making fun of my Eastern practices, like putting their hands together in prayer, bowing while repeating "Om"—with their faces grimaced in pain. I chose to brush off their insensitivity, instead concentrating on what I was learning and how I was facing life as it presented itself.

The Ram workshops and the gatherings in Rome took on a whole new meaning after my Shaktipat experience with Baba. How I viewed daily happenings changed. I was much more able to accept the challenges, the ups and downs. I was learning to examine my actions to see if they were in alignment with my world views.

After meeting Baba in Oakland, a new Ashram opened in an old hotel in the Catskill Mountains. I visited the Ashram on weekends, and then immersed myself in the practices during the month of September 1981, taking a month's vacation from work.

I began to see clearly that what was presented to me symbolized what I needed to learn. Situations and persons in my life represented my Karma, my destiny, with its attendant opportunity to transcend difficult times. I had the free will to learn, or not, and to act appropriately. I had the free will to choose. My heart opened.

I learned a lesson about acting appropriately while observing a doctor treating a patient in an emergency situation in Utica, New York, near my home.

One night late, at 11 p.m., I received a call that one of my employees, Chris, survived a serious automobile accident but was in critical condition. Because this young man did not have any family nearby, a colleague and I went to the hospital to see what we could do. When we arrived in the emergency room, Chris was lying in bed, unconscious, body in spasms, head covered in blood.

Where is the doctor?" I yelled, assuming a role of authority, since no family was there and no nurses were in sight. "Why isn't anyone paying any attention to him?"

After I found out the doctor's name, I called Barbara at home, a nurse friend who practiced at the hospital. She told me that the doctor had a good reputation and she assumed he was doing everything he could.

Shortly after I spoke with Barbara, the doctor came to see Chris, lovingly looking at him, examining the x-rays—back and forth.

The doctor explained, "Because of the extent of damage to Chris' brain, there is nothing we can do. If Chris wants to live for the next few days, he has to do it himself. There is nothing the medical community can do."

I sat there with tears in my eyes, not quite believing what I heard. Couldn't they at least try, I thought. What does it mean that Chris 'has to do it himself'?

A few days later, at the age of 25, Chris died as the result of an automobile accident, caused by a flatbed truck pulling in front of him to make a U-turn on a four-lane highway.

I've thought often about the doctor assessing the situation and determining that there was nothing he could do. What a terrible decision he had to make—to do nothing, to leave a life to fate. Chris was in charge, not the doctor.

I was learning when to take charge, and when it was best not to take charge. Recognizing when to leave a situation to fate requires a high state of consciousness.

I was gaining this sense of right action—how best to choose and perform actions according to my Dharma, following the feeling of rightness.

Through my spiritual practices I learned how to recognize a contracted state within myself, and to make choices aligning with a clearer vision of what was true. Instead of an egocentric reaction to a situation, I was recognizing when a higher path was possible and practical.

During a health scare, I had an experience of letting go, as related in one of my journals:

> One night two weeks ago I developed severe palpitations of the heart, coupled with chest pressure. I was sure I was having a heart attack. During the night, I had periods of dream sleep, meditation, depression, and a panic feeling like I might die but that would be OK—because it was my time.
>
> The next day I went to the hospital and stayed overnight while they did a battery of tests. They found nothing.
>
> Since being at the Ashram in September, I had the feeling that my life is running out. In a few years there will be no need for this body or personality. My daughter Jodi is doing fine living with her father. We have a good relationship. In a few years she will be in college and on her own.
>
> Bruce and I have a special bonding, which I think we both could let go of.
>
> Since I became involved in Yoga, I've done extremely well in my professional career. It feels like that need to be "successful" will have been lived out in a couple of years.

A few years later, my life as I knew it was over in many ways—I no longer had a secure job with a steady income. Jodi was becoming more independent, forging her own life in prep school and college, at Syracuse University. The relationship between Bruce and me was maturing—we were supporting each other's independent lives.

In the meantime, after Baba died, Gurumayi Chidvalasananda became his successor and spent much of her time at the Catskill Ashram, where I continued to visit.

Giving and Receiving

As you continue to do selfless service,
your surrender to seva becomes deeper and deeper.
You want to do seva not because you have to,
but because it creates a pond of nectar, a river of love.
—Baba Muktananda

I began to find joy in letting go, and in understanding that so much can be learned through the challenges that were presented—if my mind became free of old perceptions. Doing intense spiritual practices at the Ashram in the Catskill Mountains helped me get rid of those old perceptions, those samskaras, past impressions from previous thoughts and actions. I no longer felt the pressure of living up to the societal expectation of being a good suburban housewife. My guilt over leaving my daughter with her father was subsiding. My ability to live in the present, and to look forward rather than backward, increased.

The yogic practices freed me to choose a path true to my nature, to follow my heart.

Volunteering to work around the Ashram provided some of the best opportunities to learn about letting go of old, worn-out habits and choosing my own path. I learned so much from this selfless service, called seva, that enhanced my *sadhana*, my spiritual path.

Seva is the practice of performing work from the highest without a desire for personal gain, a detached way of being in the moment. Being absorbed in work as seva was meditation. When I gave the task-at-hand everything, no detail seemed too small or mundane, and was done with dignity.

As Baba said, "Even if you work in McDonalds and cook hamburgers, if you do it with all your being, with love, you are doing service to the universe. The doing will bring you peace."

The seva work helped to keep the Ashram operating. The jobs varied from washing dishes, to chopping vegetables, to vacuuming the Ashram lobby, to serving as a hostess for the programs in the meditation hall. Work in a spiritual space provided an opportunity for me to give back, with gratitude, for all the gifts I received while visiting and living at the Ashram in the Catskills.

One of my first seva jobs included washing off the tables in the dining room.

Maybe no one will notice if I don't remove this greasy spot, I thought as I surveyed the dining room to see if anyone was looking. It will take more time than I am willing to spend. I want to go to the chant this evening and I have the rest of the tables to clean.

Then I remembered—*I'm in an Ashram. I'm an adult, expected to do my best.* I finished wiping off the table with great care and felt pretty good. I cleaned the remaining tables and arrived at the chant on time.

I carried this awareness to my daily life to do the best I could at work and home. I learned to consciously do my work to the best of my ability without the expectation of reward or punishment. These lessons translated into my job. I began working harder, with more diligence.

I continued to visit the Ashram in the Catskills for a number of years—it was fun, and I learned so much that could be applied to my daily life.

However, I experienced major concerns with the way seva assignments reflected the roles men and women played in the outside world.

"It doesn't seem right," I said to my roommate at the Ashram. "Why do men hold more responsible positions in management than women, especially seeing there are more women here than men. I am going to see what I can do about that."

I sought opportunities to find my place *inside* the life of the

Ashram, just as I was finding my place in the world outside of the Ashram. I looked around to see what jobs might challenge me, drawn primarily to those held by men, mirroring my professional life.

Spending only periodic weekends and a few weeks there in the summer, I knew any management role would not be practical, or even possible. I lacked the skills to do traditional male jobs of carpentry and electrical work.

I searched to find a different seva after spending a month of arranging flowers and cleaning up after courses in program halls, which were both traditional female roles.

"What do you think about me driving a shuttle bus around the Ashram?" I asked my roommate. "All the drivers are now males. I would be the first woman."

In keeping with the years of working with men, I found this opportunity welcoming.

The Ashram expanded during the mid '80s to include two additional hotels in the vicinity of the original hotel. One of the converted hotels housed a main dining room, another a large meditation hall and an outdoor pavilion. All of the hotel sites accommodated people who stayed as briefly as one night to as long as a few years. During holiday weekends, over 3000 people might spend the night at the Ashram.

I approached the manager of the Transportation Department with the request, "I'd like to be a shuttle-bus driver. Do you have any openings?"

"Yes I do. We would welcome a female driver," he responded. "You will need a commercial driver's license to drive our buses." They loaned me a bus to practice, and for my driving test in nearby Monticello. The other bus drivers helped me study for the written test. I felt so proud when I passed and joined the male enclave.

So my main seva in the late '80s was to drive a shuttle bus around to the various facilities at the Ashram, primarily to take the ashramites to their sleeping accommodations, to the dining rooms, and to classes and meditation programs. I found this seva rich and rewarding.

I met many interesting visitors from around the world as they partook in various activities.

I loved with more pride than a detached yogi should experience when my fellow spiritual seekers got on the bus and exclaimed, "Oh, it is great to have a woman driver." I felt joy in knowing I chose this job that affirmed my independent nature.

Delivering my fellow ashramites to their various destinations by piloting a refurbished school bus brought on a feeling of energy flowing through me. Women, men, girls, and boys of all ages, who came from all over the United States and the world, rode the shuttle buses. Children laughed and cried; parents spoke to them with love in many different languages; singles sat quietly looking out the window; newcomers asked questions about the happenings around the Ashram; old-timers hurried on and off the bus, anxious to get to their next activity, to a meal, to a program.

This mixture of people, with their specific needs, boarded the bus as individuals or in groups. I'd drive them to one or two places, they'd get off, others would get on, some would get off at the next stop, and I'd pick others up. The cycle continued until my two to three-hour shift was over.

Sometimes I'd take a break to mitigate the high state I was experiencing. I felt such a connection with the people, the road, the woods, that I had a hard time keeping my mind focused on the task of driving the bus. The high was similar to what I felt after becoming totally absorbed in a chant in the meditation hall.

A few of the other bus drivers played chants while they drove the people around the Ashram sites. I did not because the chants just enhanced the high. I had trouble concentrating on the task at hand, wanting instead to go into a state of meditation.

The feeling of a flow of energy manifested in sweet ways when I took a course on the Bhakti Sutras.[56] One day the teacher spoke of sharing God's love, of giving and receiving.

After this teaching, while I drove during lunchtime, a young boy stepped onto the bus and said, "Thank you for driving. Here, would you like this?" He handed me a beautiful yellow rose.

With a lump in my throat over this loving gesture, I held out my hand to accept his lovely gift.

After my driving shift ended, I walked back to the course meeting room along the path in the woods, holding the rose in my hands as I admired its beauty. I visualized placing this exquisite flower at the foot of my meditation cushion at the course.

Suddenly, however, I felt a pull to offer the rose to Shiva as I passed by his statue on the edge of the footpath.

Contracted, a part of me said, "No, keep it for yourself. The boy gave it to you."

Then I remembered the teaching from the morning: "Share God's love." As I placed the offering of the rose on the stone in front of the Shiva statue, I felt a weight lifted, with the love flowing from the boy to Shiva through me. I let go of the desire to selfishly hold on to this precious gift. My heart opened.

The boy gave the rose to me with love, I took it with love, and

A statue of Shiva

then gave it to Shiva with love. The flow of love in the Ashram became a reality to me once again.

I experienced great joy witnessing the drama of other ashramites and not having to become involved in their lives.

One night while driving the shuttle bus late, I transported people who had recently arrived. They needed to take the bus from the registration area to the buildings where they were to sleep.

Included in the group that I picked up that night was a woman in a wheelchair, a woman with an autistic child, and a couple from France who had not had anything to eat. It was 10:30 p.m. and no food was available. In addition, an older woman approached the bus, looked up at me as I sat in the driver's seat, and said with a panicked look on her face, "I'm going to be sick, where is the ladies room?"

I stayed calm as I took care of their needs and reflected on the verse from the Bhagavad Gita: "The Self does not take on the sin or merit of any." I saw these people as individual selves with their own karma that I needn't take on as my own burden.

I could serve them and not be engulfed in their trials and tribulations.

I saw clearly that what was presented to me both in and out of the Ashram was a gift, often in the form of a challenge that provided an opportunity to overcome obstacles in my path. Doing seva of driving the bus at the Ashram provided me with numerous lessons in helping to recognize what is right action in mastering the subtleties and applying the principles to my life.

My life in the Ashram and my life in Rome complemented each other—the spiritual became practical, the practical, spiritual.

- - - - -

The conflicts with my boss (Jim) provided the opportunity to examine and apply lessons I learned from my spiritual experiences, so I took those practices and applied them to the problems at work. Viewing my professional job as a form of seva supported me through the rough times and guided me in acting from the center, rather than from false pride.

The decision to approach the president came from this process.

It felt true to my nature to take direct action rather than passively accept Jim's behavior. Overcoming the ambush in the basement of his suburban home meant purging resentment toward him while fighting for what I felt was right for my career and the company. I gained the strength to stop complaining and gossiping with my colleagues about my problems.

I am filled with gratitude for this yogic path that supported me in dealing with such difficult events. I surrendered and let go of the organization that I helped make a success.

I wrote to Ram: "More than ever, I'm feeling that things are just happening to me as they should, and I don't have to do anything except keep in tune with the present. Who knows what will happen tomorrow."

I chose to start my own computer software consulting business as the next phase of my career, confident in my ability to move forward.

Not Seeing Clearly

Once a monkey squeezed its hand through a jar with a narrow neck to get the banana that was inside. As it fell onto the banana, its fist was too large to pull out of the jar. It pulled and pulled, but its hand wouldn't come out. Neither would it let go of the banana. It was determined to hold on.

Many of us are like the monkey. We hold on to so many things that keep us bound. We live in prisons of our own creation.

—Correspondence Course, Ram Butler

In late 1987, shortly after I started my consulting company, I attended a computer conference in San Francisco, planning to fly to Los Angeles for a meeting the next week with a new client, the Jet Propulsion Laboratory in Pasadena, California.

Having a weekend free on the West Coast between the computer conference and the client meeting afforded the opportunity to spend a couple of days at the Ashram in Oakland, the same place where I had met Baba Muktananda eight years before.

After the end of the conference on Friday, I drove the rental car across the Bay Bridge from San Francisco to Oakland. Registration was not open when I arrived at the Ashram, so I went to Marina Park, at the end of Powell Street in nearby Emeryville, to wait until I could register to stay at the Ashram for the weekend.

Located on the north side of San Francisco Bay, Marina Park is spectacular since it overlooks the city and the Golden Gate Bridge. The park was crowded that Friday afternoon with people walking, jogging, and strolling with their dogs on the multiple paths leading to and alongside San Francisco Bay. I found a parking spot in the almost full lot, locked my purse, briefcase, and suitcase in the trunk, and went for a walk by the water.

I began to feel vulnerable after about ten minutes walking alone in the park, looking around to see if there were any suspicious men who might be stalking me. I tried some calming thoughts—Why should I be scared with so many people around? It is not as if I am on a lonely road somewhere. And my car is locked, so that should be OK.

But the neighborhood in Oakland is questionable, I reasoned. Feeling unsafe, I walked back along the paths to the parking lot.

When I returned to my rental car, I noticed a white panel truck parked close to the driver's side of my car, such that I had difficulty opening the door. I noticed the man in the passenger seat of the van holding something in his lap. I looked away as I thought he might be masturbating.

Once inside the car, I admonished myself for being afraid, reasoning that my prejudice was showing because many of the people in the park were African American.

I won't be intimidated. I'll be brave. I'll go for another walk, I told myself as I opened the car door just enough to squeeze out, not looking at the two passengers in the white panel truck still parked next to my car.

I made the wrong decision.

I returned to the car about a half-hour later to a broken window on the driver's side, the trunk ajar, and no purse or briefcase in the trunk. A lonely suitcase remained.

I admonished myself. Why had I left? I'd *known* something was wrong and had not taken steps to take care of myself. That suspicious white panel truck should not have been parked so close—the man who looked guilty in the passenger seat had a rock, or some other instrument, that was used to break the window.

Mostly I cried, feeling vulnerable and alone. I was woman-as-victim, a role I tried avoiding most of my adult life. I had not empowered myself.

My only possessions were keys to the rental car in my pocket and the suitcase in the trunk. I had no purse, no money, no credit cards, and no driver's license.

Tears ran down my cheeks as I drove to a nearby restaurant to use their telephone. With voice shaking, I called to report the robbery to the police and the credit card company. I had trouble getting any words out when I spoke to Bruce, seeking support and sympathy.

I sat in the car in the restaurant parking lot, overwhelmed with uncertainty, not knowing what to do without any money, without any form of identification, admonishing myself for my lack of smarts. Why had I not driven away when I first went back to the car? Why did I not follow my intuition? Why had I not internalized the outward signs?

All my materials for the meeting with my client were gone. If only they had just taken my purse and not my briefcase, I lamented. They could have my money, but the slides and notes for my meeting next week were gone. My computer at home contained all the materials—3,000 miles away. I had no secretary or colleagues or anyone who could reconstruct what I needed for the meeting.

The thought of the comfort of the Ashram brought relief. People in the Oakland Ashram might provide me with support, which they did in the form of food and lodging for the night, with some cash for my return trip on Saturday. Bruce was able to book me on a flight home the next day. I rescheduled my business meeting to the following week.

Surface anxiety waned as the practicalities were effectively met. It was the deep-seated fear and vulnerability that needed to be dissipated. That feeling of woman-as-victim was ever present.

I did not want the negativities towards the men to fester, the resentments to become so deep that they would stay, bothering me for years to come. I shared those sentiments with a friend in the Ashram, remembering how the power of chanting and meditation had helped to release negativity toward Jim.

I felt a release of anxiety during the chanting and meditation program in the Ashram hall that Friday evening.

The hall was filled with Shakti, the spiritual energy accumulated from the meditation practices of many spiritual seekers over the years. Chanting loosened my negative thoughts. The practices did their job, preventing the afternoon experiences from getting stuck and becoming deep-seated samskaras.

Strength returned to me in this protected environment.

A threatening dream that night in the Ashram dormitory helped in the release:

> A large dark cloud encompassed my vision with the form of a human being faintly visible inside the cloud. The dark cloud and human form slowly melted away, leaving a background of soft white light.

When I awoke most of the fear and anxiety had gone.

The trip home on Saturday presented few challenges.

I did, however, have to keep reminding the people at the rental car agency when I returned the car at the airport, "I have no cash, no credit card, no driver's license, no way to prove that I am myself—I was just robbed." The same small annoyances occurred at the airport when I picked up the return plane ticket that Bruce had reserved and paid for with his credit card. After explaining my situation and getting the ticket from the agent, all I had to do was walk to the gate and board the plane. Bruce and Jodi met me with open arms at the gate at the Syracuse airport.[57]

Looking back at my decision to go for another walk instead of driving away in the parking lot in Oakland, I realize my mind was cluttered with the need to be macho, to fight my instincts.

I was bound to the notion that, as a woman, I should not buckle under potential threats.

Instead I should have known that the smart and brave action would have been to leave the scene of danger. I did not always follow my instincts or my insights into the happenings around me.

I did not always choose the right path.

Part V

Choosing a Path

Life After 50

From the wise old pinnacle of my years,
I can tell you that what you're looking for is already inside you.
—Anne Lamott

I knew I needed to examine what I wanted to do with the rest of my life, or at least what direction I could see for myself in the near future. It was my 50th year and I wanted something more fulfilling professionally. Traveling was getting to be a bore. I was not willing to do, or interested in doing, what was necessary to earn lots of money. I just wanted to be comfortable.

I contemplated my true needs, using the tools I had learned in yoga to penetrate below the surface ring of thoughts that circled in my mind. I followed the advice Baba Muktananda gave to Ram when Ram asked him about a path he should take.

> Do what you want to do.
> Do what is convenient.
> Do what is your true nature.

I reflected on these issues, wrote in my journals, spoke with my yoga buddies and other friends. Mostly, I let the questions sit inside of me and jell.

It became clear that I wanted to live an independent life, free of the requirements of a corporate career. I liked what university life had to offer—the prestige, the interaction with academics, the sharing of ideas. Pursuing a Ph.D. would meet a need I'd had for years to do research on problems the software industry encountered while developing computer software and the challenge to enhance the usability of such systems.

My draw to live in the Adirondacks was becoming more intense as the years went by. I wanted a cabin in the woods in the Adirondacks, to live in the peace and quiet of the mountains and lakes in this sacred place I had learned to love.

In January 1989, I began the Ph.D. program at the School of Information Studies at Syracuse University, delaying the cabin in the woods for a later time.

I sold my house in Rome and bought another one in Syracuse to be near the university.

A research assistant position from the university paid a minimalist stipend and covered full tuition. Continued consulting jobs provided enough money to minimize the need to dip into my savings.

I went to the Ashram in Ganeshpuri, India, for two weeks to help bless my new life.

India Lessons

*Two hundred fifty-nine people on the plane and eleven people
on the ground were killed as a result of the explosion. Four
hundred parents lost a child, 46 parents lost their only child,
65 women were widowed, 11 men lost their wives, 140 people
lost a parent, and seven lost both parents.*[58]

I traveled to India for two weeks in December 1988 to
accumulate blessings before beginning my new life as a student in a
Ph.D. program at Syracuse University, fearful of the future because
of a decrease in my standard of living. I felt anxious about keeping
up with my fellow students who were much younger than my 50
years. I sought an auspicious start for my new ventures. Taking this
pilgrimage to India represented a way to welcome the Shakti, the
spiritual energy, to help protect and provide strength as I ventured
forth in this new life quest.

I arrived at Baba's Ashram in Ganeshpuri, India, early in the
morning after a flight from Kennedy Airport to Bombay, India,
passing through Heathrow Airport in London. I was tired but happy
to finally visit the Ashram after hearing all the stories about this
sacred place from Baba, Gurumayi, Ram, and my fellow seekers.

Challenges to my living arrangements showed the way to a
difficult time ahead. I had trouble sleeping on a hard bed in a hot,
crowded dormitory with nine other women, some who snored
loudly. The heat of the day overwhelmed me—I had chosen to come
in December, hoping it would not be oppressive, but it was.

The exotic tropical flowers, bushes, and trees around the
beautiful grounds of the Ashram were in sharp contrast to the

dilapidated, corrugated-tin houses and the grinding poverty outside of the gates. The abject poverty overwhelmed me.

"Did you see all the open sewage running throughout the dirt streets?" I asked my roommate. Continuing with amazement, "But the people I saw living in this poverty seemed happy, with smiles all around." Who was I to judge what was good or bad.

I experienced many such contrasts in India.

It took me a number of days to accept the challenges of living in the Ashram. Once over the shock of my resistances, I began to accept the heat, the noise, and the poverty. I learned that yogurt cooled you, chocolate made you hot; the meditation cave had air-conditioning, making it a good place to meditate in the afternoon; earplugs helped with snoring roommates; and the faces of the people living in the poverty outside of the Ashram looked more peaceful than some in the Ashram, including myself.

I had to remind myself—I am in the Ashram to have an auspicious start for my new ventures. If I am resisting the Shakti in the Ashram, how well will I be able to accept the challenges ahead in my Ph.D. program?

Once I relaxed, I was OK and could appreciate the beauty of the grounds and the people. Chanting was ecstatic.

Meditations brought peace and clarity to the way forward. My time at the Ashram did give me some much-needed grounding that would prove important.

I knew that keeping up a solid meditation and chanting practice would help me stay centered on my studies. I suspected that being a lowly student, down many rungs on the ladder from my pedestal as manager of over 100 people, would be a challenge. I needed the wisdom to imbibe the teachings of detachment and integrity to keep my independent spirit in the role of a humble student.

However, the immediacy of the trip home presented its own challenges.

December 21, 1988, the taxi picked me up at the Ashram at three o'clock in the morning, destined for the airport in Bombay, 40 miles away. My throat tightened and eyes watered as the taxi

Chanting with a group, my favorite practice

weaved in and out between the trucks on the two-lane dirt roads, the exhaust streaming into the taxi windows. I sat in the back seat, stopped in traffic with a rock cliff protruding into the road on my left, a livestock truck exuding fumes on the right. I thought, I am in a cave centered in hell. How am I going to get out?

What a contrast to the oasis I had left just an hour before—the lush gardens of the Ashram and the melodic chants that permeated every pore of the meditators.

Once at the Bombay airport, I entered the business-class lounge, thankful the taxi ride was over and grateful I had spent the money to upgrade to business class. I knew that the flights from Bombay, to New Delhi, to London's Heathrow airport, and New York's John F. Kennedy airport constituted a marathon journey. Twenty hours in the air was the original projected time frame.

Halfway from Bombay to New Delhi, the pilot announced, "The New Delhi airport is fogged in and we must return to Bombay." No more information than that.

On our return to Bombay, passengers traded fears about what this setback would do to our schedules. Our Air India itinerary required a change of planes in New Delhi, with a stop in London on our way to New York. A bad start to a very long trip.

Back in the Bombay airport, no alternative flight plans were offered from our original schedule. Disembarked passengers yelled while crowding around the lone ticket agent, demanding passage to their destinations. To help relieve brewing boredom, I followed the antics of one of the passengers with whom I had spoken earlier, a 30-ish New York City-bound American dressed as if he were ready to attend a board meeting. My taking part in the chaos began as entertainment. However, I retreated as I sensed violence brewing. The negative energy weighed heavily on my quickly tiring body.

Returning to the lounge, I unwound, commiserating with my fellow passengers who had also settled into passivity. Suddenly the door to the lounge opened, and the well-dressed New York City-bound American yelled, "I don't know what you people want to do, but I just got a flight to London! They told us to board. If you want to stay here, OK. I'm going." We glanced at each other, realizing that we did not even know when we were to leave for New Delhi, much less London.

Finally we boarded our plane to New Delhi, without the well-dressed New York City-bound American. We assumed he took the earlier flight to London.

By the time our plane arrived in New Delhi, we had missed our flight to London and had to wait in the New Delhi airport an additional four hours for the next flight. My body knew it was 50 years old with the difficulty of trying to sleep on the hard chairs in the public area, for the New Delhi airport had no business-class lounge.

I settled into my seat on the flight from New Delhi to London with a feeling of rightness. Reflecting on the scene of the screaming crowd at the ticket counter in the Bombay airport, I knew in my heart that removing myself was something I needed to do. After all, from my time at the Ashram, I hoped I had learned how to discriminate between what was good for me and what was harmful.

The Indian food in the business-class section of the plane tasted comforting, and sleeping came easily. I did not have to worry about connecting flights since our plane just stopped in London on the way to New York. I wondered if the distraught fellow-American passenger in Bombay had already reached his New York destination.

Eleven hours late, we arrived at London's Heathrow Airport, at about 9 p.m. I visited the in-flight lounge to stretch my legs while waiting for the plane to take off for Kennedy.

The scene inside the lounge was like a disaster movie. The TV showed devastating clips of a plane crash over Lockerby, Scotland. A Pan American plane, #103, having left Heathrow for Kennedy Airport at 6:25 p.m., blew-up in midair about 40 minutes after takeoff and crashed to the ground in Scotland. The authorities expressed concern that all passengers and crew members were killed, along with people on the ground in Lockerby.

After returning to the plane and telling the other business-class passengers about the crash, we compared our initial reaction to how close we had come to disaster. Would we have made connections to Pan Am 103 if we had taken the direct Bombay-to-London flight, as possibly our fellow American passenger had done? We didn't know.

Our plane was delayed in London an extra few hours because of heightened security. Because the authorities identified one unaccounted-for piece of luggage, we all had to de-plane, then claim and recheck our luggage before the plane could leave Heathrow. Now we were approximately 15 hours late.

Bruce picked me up at Kennedy Airport that day, worried that I may have changed my plans and been on the Pan Am flight. When I walked into the arrival area, he jumped over the ropes, hugging me as hard as he ever had, happy that I had kept the original plane schedule.

I feel such gratitude for all I learned in the Ashram. The spiritual practices helped prepare me for surrendering to the futility of fighting circumstances over which I had little control. I'm glad I was able to remove myself from the aggression displayed by the passengers in Bombay. Doing so may have saved my life.

Thirty-five college students returning from London through the Syracuse University Semester-abroad program were all killed on

Pan Am #103. The connections to Syracuse made the disaster close to home, with Bruce as a professor, Jodi a senior, and me a new Ph.D. student.

Syracuse University held a memorial service for the victims of the study-abroad program after the student body returned to school from the Christmas break. Even though I had started my studies at Syracuse, I did not attend the service, when most everyone else I knew at the university did. Perhaps I felt survivor's guilt. Perhaps I was not ready to mourn in such a public way, needing a more personal experience, which came a few years later.

In the fall of 1995, Dark Elegy, a collection of sculptures created by Suse Lowenstein, mother of one of the Pan Am victims, was brought to the university campus. It consists of 75 individual sculptures that depicted women, mothers, and wives during the first moments when they learned of their loss.

I experienced such a wrenching sadness as I viewed the Dark Elegy sculptures when it came to Syracuse that fall. Briefly, I felt a deep emptiness enter me. Then I saw the beauty of how Lowenstein captured this moment and how much her sculptures could help the women in their grieving process.

The bombing of Pan Am 103 was the loss of our country's innocence, the deadliest attack on American civilians until September 11, 2001.

Such a seemingly insignificant choice to act on my own behalf kept me from being one of them.

The Ph.D. Process

We have the freedom to go our own way, if we choose.
—Noam Chomsky

I chose to leave the business world to pursue a Ph.D. because I wanted to expand my horizons. Even though I knew I would pay an enormous price financially, I felt the need to chart a new direction that would bring growth and, hopefully, joy to the next 15 or so productive years of my life.

My financial obligation to Jodi's college was just ending as she graduated from Syracuse with a bachelor's degree in mathematics, just a few months after I began my studies.

Returning to school at the age of 50, taking direction from professors often younger than me, and studying with students fresh out of a master's program humbled me. I entered the Ph.D. program in the School of Information Studies (IST) at Syracuse expecting incorrectly that my years in the computer software field and management experience would ensure an easy path through my studies. I was wrong.

I sat in class realizing that my years of managing a group of software engineers actually was a liability rather than a benefit. So much of my day during the last ten years had been spent dealing with the personnel issues of over 100 employees, managing finances, and meeting with clients.

I lacked current computer skills, given the fast-changing nature of computer technology.

My mind had forgotten how to delve deeply into a subject. I did not know how to study.

I chose a program of study concentrated on enriching my

Jodi and Lorraine at Jodi's graduation

knowledge to better understand how to design and develop computer software that was easy to use by the end user, especially those who had little knowledge of or interest in computer technology. This goal required taking course work in behavioral and cognitive science, mapping and geography, and human-computer interaction. Some required courses were difficult for me. With a math background, I was horrified that I experienced problems in mastering the statistics taught—I almost failed the first statistics course.

My statistics professor called me into his office one day, explaining his process in grading tests. "The first time I look at the name of the student is *after* I have determined their grade. In looking at your test paper, I hoped the student was not in our Ph.D. program, and was disappointed to see it was you."

I looked down at the floor and felt my face flush.

He continued, "I was kind and gave you a C grade. What can we do to have you better understand?"

I was mortified. A grade of C in graduate school is like an F in undergraduate programs. I needed to take another look at how I was going to get through this program of study.

I started asking for the assistance of my fellow students and professors.

I asked the smartest person in the class, "Carol, may I study with you and Mike? I don't understand the assignment." My favorite professor, Liz, helped to chart a course of study that built upon my current knowledge. I kept reminding myself, You are no longer the fast-charging manager with employees willing and able to do what you want. You no longer have your own secretary, no one to give assignments to. You have to do it all yourself.

Coming from a place of authority to one of submission took its toll. Thankfully, with coursework completed, I could now chart my own direction.

"What are you going to do for your dissertation?" Ann asked, knowing I was nearing completion of my course work for my Ph.D. at Syracuse University. How relieved I felt hearing that question, sensing an end to the arduous and sometimes demeaning tasks—at least for me—required through my course of study.

"I'm settling on the main thread for my dissertation," I told Ann. "I am doing a qualitative study on the problems of software managers in a multitude of development environments for a variety of applications. So far I have lined up interviews with managers at IBM, General Electric, Eastman Kodak, and ATT Bell Laboratories."

Ann seemed interested so I continued; "I need a way to add some punch; I'm thinking about interviewing some managers in Japan. No one has ever compared the problems managers have in Japan with those in the US."

"That sounds great," replied Ann. "Koji and Kishida"—two colleagues from Japan—"are here and you could talk with them."

We were attending an international software engineering conference in a hotel in Los Angeles at the time, sponsored by the Computer Society. I had been on the board of the Computer Society a few years before, and the chair of one of their technical committees, so I knew the gentlemen Ann mentioned. I had also hosted a few of their Japanese colleagues five years before at our offices in Rome. I knew they had sponsored other researchers in the past and were likely candidates to be interested in such a study.

At the next coffee break at the conference, I approached Koji and Kishida with my proposal to interview software managers in Japan.

They looked at each other, smiled, nodded, and said, "Sure, let's talk about it." My heart started beating so fast. I was on the one hand elated, and on the other not wanting to depend on this snap-decision they had just made. Remember, I said to myself, the Japanese often say yes just to be polite. They may mean no.

I cautiously congratulated myself: my years of setting up an international network of colleagues was coming to fruition.[59] This would be so great.

Great it was—more than I would ever have hoped. I spent three months as a visiting professor at Osaka University. I interviewed over 22 managers—all men—in Osaka and Tokyo, representing automobile manufacturers (Toshiba), Japanese electronic manufacturers (Hitachi, NEC, and Mitsubishi Electric Corporation), and Japanese subsidiaries of US computer manufacturers (IBM and Unisys).[60]

My hosts, Koji Torii from Osaka University and Kouichi Kishida from Software Research Associates, supplied me with office space at the university and a Western-style studio apartment in nearby Esaka.[61]

They were proud of the apartment because it had a modern kitchenette, a full bathroom, and a bed for sleeping. The older, Japanese-style apartments might only include a few burners for cooking, possibly a toilet, and a futon folded up during the day and placed on a tatami mat for sleeping at night. Central bathroom facilities would be shared with the apartment complex.

I commuted every day to the university on a subway and bus, stopping at night on the way home to pick up food for dinner and breakfast. I normally went to lunch at the university with a mixture of professors and students—all men.

The status of women in Japan in 1992 reminded me of the yearning I felt 30 years earlier in my Manhattan apartment reading *The Feminine Mystique,* illustrated now by the desire of a young Japanese woman in a short story in an English-language weekly magazine.[62]

> Most of the time I just want to slither down and let happen what may, but something keeps pushing me to look for a better way.
>
> Not that I want to save the world or become president of Mitsubishi, or anything like that. I just want to control my own destiny. I want to live my life the way I want to live it, not the way someone else wants me to live it.

I was living my life the way I wanted by pursuing a Ph.D. and doing research in Japan for my dissertation. I was controlling my

Lorraine joins with her Japanese colleagues for a sushi feast

own destiny, pleased to learn that Asian women were becoming aware of their needs, even though they were about 40 years behind the feminist movement in Western countries.

Maggie, a visiting researcher from Massachusetts, and Sanji, Koji's secretary, were the only two women I would interact with on a daily basis at the university.

Every afternoon at the university, Sanji, dressed in a white, starched apron, served English tea to the professors, delivered directly to our desks. Embarrassed with this show of servitude, Maggie and I expressed our disapproval of this custom and refused the tea service. Sanji, as was true of most Japanese women I encountered, seldom spoke directly to others unless spoken to first. She'd hold her head down, giggle a lot, and place her hand over her mouth, speaking in

Koji and Sanji

a soft voice, almost a whisper.

Women in Japan held the positions of secretary, clerical office workers, and sales women in retail stores, and quit when they got married. There were very few professional women. I saw no professors of engineering or computer science. Few graduate students.

The job of airline stewardess was revered in Japan.

In the late '80s and early '90s, English schools across Japan provided stewardess training classes, since few jobs for women offered the salary, travel, and glamour status of the working stewardess.

"The status of stewardesses is very high in Japanese society," says Inoue Takehiko, school principal of Fuji Gakuin. "If young women work for an ordinary company, they just help their male colleagues. They don't have a job of their own. As a stewardess they can do their own work, wear an attractive uniform, and earn a high salary."[63]

In 1991, 9533 women applied for 600 positions at one of the Japanese airlines.

During my visit to Japan, I was surprised to meet an assertive Japanese woman at a university New Year's party. She approached me, stating emphatically, "I hate coming back to Japan because of the way we are treated here; the status of women is so low. What has been your experience?"

She graduated a few years earlier with a Computer Science master's degree from Osaka University, and almost immediately moved to the United States, working for an American company. She returned home to Japan for the holidays.

"I think the status of women in Japan is about what it was like in the mid to late '60s in the United States; maybe before, similar to the 1950s," I replied. "However, Japan may be changing faster than we did in the US because of the role models the rest of the world have provided you."

I came to that conclusion after reading stories in English-language magazines and newspapers. For example, a woman director of the International Counseling Centre in Kobe shared this insight in a 1992 magazine article.[64]

> I finally decided to tell Sei that I wasn't going to marry him. I wanted to work and make my own life, my own way.
> I also decided to take my American friend Ellen's advice, and get tough as nails and start kicking ass, as she puts it, in the office.

This experience of living in Japan helped me to recognize the progress we had made in the United States in our treatment of women. We still had a ways to go but had come so far.

- - - - -

After returning to the United States and completing my dissertation, I worked for a few years with a computer technology company, saving enough money so I could pursue my dream of living in the Adirondacks, a pursuit that had begun with vacation trips years ago.

Part VI

Thriving

The Adirondack Dream Fulfilled

What you get by achieving your goals is not as important
as what you become by achieving your goals.
—Henry David Thoreau

"I found a motel," I whispered to Jodi as she lay asleep in the back seat of the car in the early summer of 1975.

We experienced the isolation of the wildness of the Adirondack Park as I drove with Jodi, my seven-year old daughter, on a deserted, two-lane road. We were traveling from Syracuse, now several hours to the south, and it had grown late and dark. Wilderness surrounded us on all sides as I searched anxiously for a motel, B&B—*any place* where we could stay for the night. But the area was remote. Stretches of cold, gray mountains, covered in pine, balsam and hardwood forests. I thought we would find a motel on the way, close to Utica, but as we drove toward Speculator, I found nothing.

What a poor job I did planning this trip, I bitterly admonished myself. How could I have forgotten how deserted Route 8 is from Utica northward to the south-central part of the Adirondacks?

I knew driving alone at night in the wilderness would be a challenge. I thrived on adventures that tested my abilities, mentally and physically. But had I pushed myself and my independent streak too far this time, considering my small daughter was in tow? The torturous week at work had left me fatigued. Would I be able to handle any challenges that might suddenly come up should I find us stranded on the highway or unable to find a place for the night? Sometimes, maybe, I put myself too far out on a limb.

Mile after mile, our headlights shone on the empty road ahead, as evening dusk became the pitch-dark of a wilderness night.

With a huge sense of relief, the headlights finally lit up a sign, one that said Oxbow Motel. But the buildings were dark, except for a small, lighted office sign in the window of the main building.

Pulling quickly into the lot, I knocked on the door, pleading with the owner to give us a place to stay for the night. He gave us a small, cozy room overlooking the lake.

That night, laying awake, I thought about how as the years went by, my pull to the Adirondacks had intensified. Now that I was living in upstate New York again, after having spent nine years in the Midwest as a married woman, the opportunities to immerse myself in the mountains were at hand.

But would I be able to find what I was looking for—not just property-wise, but in my spirit? I thought about Mrs. Hawkins, back in my neighborhood when I was growing up. Had she ever found her own personal "*somewhere*, over the rainbow"? Had life in the neighborhood as someone's wife, someone's mom, been enough for her? Or had she dreamed … and did she ever find the rainbow's-end of those dreams? Would I find mine?

And what exactly *was* my dream for myself now, at this stage of my life?

The morning brought me back to the present.

"I'm hungry, Mommy," Jodi whispered when she woke up early. With no restaurants or convenience stores around, I hurriedly checked out of the motel and drove to Speculator, to the one restaurant open for breakfast in the village.

As we ate breakfast, I marveled at the beauty of Lake Pleasant, excited to be back in this beautiful, six-million-acre Adirondack Park wilderness with its expanse of forests and pristine waters. I loved being back here, feeling the thrill of a remote area, of seeing woods and waters and mountains free of 24-hour convenience stores, of signs of civilization.

I wanted Jodi to experience this growing love I had for the Adirondack Park. I wanted it to open up her mind, her heart, and soul to the serenity that comes with the spirit of the place.

This pull to a place—the Adirondacks—where my heart felt at home, began so many years before, in the summer of 1949, when we Girl Scouts went on the canoe trip to Upper Saranac Lake. We liked the canoe-camping in the Adirondacks so much that the next year our counselors planned a trip up the Fulton Chain of Lakes, starting in Old Forge in the southwest corner of the Park.

As I grew into adulthood—during those years of city and suburban living—something had been missing. My desire to be a part of the mountains remained, even though my visits to the Adirondacks were few.

Moving back East after the divorce, I vigorously pursued opportunities to explore different areas of the Park. I was intrigued when a feminist publication ran an article on the Woman's Retreat Center in Paradox, New York, in the eastern part of the Park, near Lake Champlain and the Vermont border.

Now, I thought, as Jodi and I finished our breakfast, spending time in the mountains with my daughter at a feminist retreat would be a good combination of three loves of mine. The night at the Oxbow Motel was a sojourn on our way to the Center.

When we arrived at the Retreat Center, two women around my age, the mid-thirties, dressed in the hippy garb of the time—long skirts and peasant blouses—greeted us and walked us to our nearby room in a rustic A-frame. One of the women whisked Jodi away, leading her to a child's playhouse where they had activities for children. I felt guilty that they took her away so quickly, but relieved that I had some alone time with adult women.

The owner of the Retreat Center, Julie, led me on a hike to a nearby pond, sharing her joy of the freedom as a recently divorced woman and the opening up of the retreat center.

I confessed, "I just got a divorce and moved back East, while my daughter is staying with her father for the school year. She is with me this summer. "

And then, quickly, I expressed my angst about leaving my only child with her father, "How could I do that? Why did I give up custody?"

To my relief, I wasn't shunned or reprimanded, as had happened in the past with my family and suburban friends. In fact, Julie shared her fear of not being a good mother, even though she had custody of her children. I cried a little, sensing that she understood my guilt and longing to do right by Jodi under the circumstances.

After about 30 minutes sitting on the rocks by the water and talking, Julie casually pulled her peasant blouse over her head, exposing her breasts, for she was not wearing a bra. She encouraged me to do the same and warm my body in the sun. I was embarrassed but went along, feeling wicked remembering when, as a Girl Scout, I went skinny-dipping with my girlfriends on a remote pond during our trip to Upper Saranac Lake.

The sun warmed my body and softened my mind. I melted into the place I loved, immersed in the freedom I felt sitting half-nude in nature on a rock by a pond, with a nurturing woman.

Experiencing such a connection with self-determined women was a big draw to the Adirondacks.

I visited the Women's Retreat two other times with my friends from Rome. I read *Woodswoman*, a memoir by Anne LaBastille, in which she told of building her own cabin and living alone in the wilderness in the Adirondacks. I attended numerous weekends at Great Camp Sagamore in the Central Adirondacks, where Anne was the featured guest at wilderness retreats for women.

Using Anne as my role model, I yearned to live in the wilderness.

I read magazines, articles, historical essays, and books, often disappointed at the lack of stories about independent Adirondack women. A macho milieu of Adirondack toughness pervaded the legends, evidenced by a quote from a pioneer visitor, William H. H. Murray, who availed himself of local guide services:

> A good guide, like a good wife, is indispensable
> to one's success, pleasure, and peace.

I wanted to learn how more women lived their lives in the Adirondacks in a softer, gentler way. I yearned to associate with

Anne sharing her experiences with us at Sagamore

other women who felt a spiritual connection to the Adirondack Mountains, lakes, forests, and sky.[65]

Searching, I found one book, *The Healing Woods* by Martha Reben, set in and around Saranac Lake in the 1930s. At first glance, I thought it might tell a tale that related to being an independent woman living in the wilderness. Instead, Martha tells her story of how she, with her male guide's assistance, spent six months on Weller Pond near Middle Saranac Lake, healing her lungs from tuberculosis. Her story did not relate to me, given my thoughts about a woman's independence. She depended on her guide, a man, for much of her survival.

I became discouraged with stories about Anne LaBastille's dependence on men. As the stories go, Anne's male neighbors helped build and maintain her cabin on the wilderness lake. The lake itself was not as remote as Anne had portrayed in her books; many camps dotted the shorelines.

I began to observe self-sufficient women as I visited the Adirondacks—not famous, but ones who had an independent streak.

One instance occurred when I was attending a computer software workshop at Syracuse University's Minnowbrook Conference Center at Blue Mountain Lake. One day, two male colleagues and I went for a walk near Lake Durant, a small, state-owned wilderness lake in the central Adirondacks near the village of Blue Mountain Lake. A woman with a small canoe on top of her car pulled up to the lake, near where we were walking. She parked, opened the door, unfastened the canoe straps, and lifted the canoe off her car. It was so lightweight she carried and handled it with ease. In short order, she placed the canoe in the water, where it glided swiftly through the gentle waves as she paddled across Lake Durant. She did this all within 5 minutes.

"I want that!" I said to my colleagues.

After the conference, I spoke with anyone who might know how she was able to handle the canoe so deftly, finding out that lightweight solo canoes were made right here in the Adirondacks. I visited the owner, Peter Hornbeck, ordered a 10.5 ft. 15 lb. Kevlar canoe, and was on the water the next spring. I loved leaving work in Utica where I was living at the time and, within a half hour, was paddling down West Canada Creek, near the town of Barneveld.

The pull to live in the energy of the Adirondack Mountains continued to intensify through the years while I lived in Rome. Bruce would not join me on any mountain sojourns. He resisted most attempts I made to include him in my interest.

I knew if I was to fulfill my desire to live in the Adirondacks, I would have to do it myself.

I attended two events, ski jumping and cross-country skiing, at the 1980 Winter Olympics in Lake Placid, then bought a timeshare condo in the village to provide me, even if I was alone, a place to spend at least one week of the year on vacation in Lake Placid, learning about this place I loved.

Not knowing anyone in the area, and fearful of hiking in the woods by myself, I hired a guide to take my daughter and me in the woods. We went up Baxter Mountain, a hike of which the guide said, "Local people come up here on their lunch hour." I felt like such a jerk to need a guide in a place that some consider their back yard. I vowed, I'm going to live like this *is* my back yard. I'm going to hike this myself, alone. I'm going to learn to not be afraid in the woods.

In 1987 I began my search for land in the Adirondacks.

I sat talking in the dining room at the Ashram in the Catskills, telling a friend about my dreams—to get a Ph.D. and a cabin in the woods in the Adirondacks. She said, "There is a man from the Yoga center in Soho that just published a book on the Adirondacks—Nathan Farb."

Paddling on West Canada Creek

"Oh great!" I replied. "I have his book. It's filled with amazing photos of the mountains, forests, and waters."

I wrote a fan letter to Nathan, the first fan letter in my life, other than to a movie star, Glenn Ford, when I was in the 8th grade:

> I am so excited to know we practice the same meditation. I love your wonderful photography book of the Adirondacks. I am hoping to live in the Adirondacks some day, and am just beginning to look for land in the High Peaks area, which is where I understand you have a place.

Unexpectedly, Nathan called on the phone to thank me, and invited me to stop by his house in Jay if I were ever in the area. Jay is in the Ausable River Valley near the foothills of the High Peaks' towns of Keene and Lake Placid.

The next spring I drove to Jay, bringing my 80-year-old mother, since she liked vacationing in the mountains.

Nathan was very polite and offered to help me find property in the area.

I delayed looking for a place in the Adirondacks for a few years while I pursued my Ph.D.

I began a serious search in 1993, working with realtors and following-up on For Sale ads in Adirondack publications. I became discouraged because finding desirable land that I could afford seemed impossible. I wanted wooded land with a view of mountains, and few neighbors. Lake property would have been nice, but I knew I could not afford a combination of water and remoteness.

During the period of searching, my daughter, her husband, and Bruce and I spent a long weekend at a B&B near where Nathan lived.

We were eating dinner at Purdy's Elm Tree Inn in Keene when, to my great delight, Nathan walked into the restaurant. Because it had been a number of years since I had seen him, I asked the bartender, and he confirmed that it was indeed Nathan Farb. By this time Nathan was quite famous, and approaching him was like hawking a celebrity. My family knew this and were embarrassed that I even considered talking to him. So they left the restaurant and I went to his table, reintroducing myself.

"Yes, I remember that you visited one time," Nathan said. "Are you still looking for land? I have 75 acres for sale five miles from the restaurant." He had purchased the land ten years previous with the hope of building a house.

"Unfortunately," he explained, "I won't be able to live there because of family obligations. But I'll keep my place in Jay."

I was thrilled. Soon after, I looked at the land and made an offer.

As it happened, the purchase agreement took a few years to complete, primarily because of logistics, for Nathan was not spending much time at his Adirondack home, and I only visited periodically. We did finally meet to complete the transaction at the property in Keene, in an area called the Glen, a flat plateau of fields

Jodi and her husband Tom

and woods surrounded by the Jay Mountain Range on the east and the Sentinel Mountain Range on the west.

The proprietor at the B&B where we stayed said, "The Glen is my favorite place in the Adirondacks. It reminds me of Montana with its open views and distant mountains. You are lucky to find something for sale there."

I experienced disbelief and gratitude as Nathan took me on a tour, starting out at a three-acre field. We walked the remaining 72-acre property, all forestland, with Nathan explaining that the beginning trail followed an old farm road, then about 50 years old. There were few farms left because the settlers found it difficult, mostly impossible, to subsist with the short growing season and the cold and snowy winters.

Sheep grazed on a portion of the property. "See the remnants of the rusted metal fences," Nathan offered.

We walked up hills, over streams, and bushwhacked through the 50-year-old boreal forest of balsam fir, white pines, spruce pine, white and yellow birches, and sugar maple trees.

Halfway through the tour, Nathan stopped at his favorite place in the woods, with a stream running on two sides below steep banks—a moraine, a peninsula consisting of sand formed during the glacier period.

Nathan sat on the ground covered with moss and pine needles, with his back resting against a white pine tree. He meditated for a few minutes, with his eyes closed and hands lying with open palms on his lap.

I remained quiet, sensing that he needed to know if I would respect the land as he did. I must have passed the test for we continued our walk, talking about finishing the transaction.

I could not believe my good fortune. My dream of living in the Adirondacks was coming to fruition.

On a rainy day a few months later, I took my aging mother to the land. She did not want to get out of the car and get wet, so I encouraged her to at least put her feet on the ground. I wanted her energy to be a part of this sacred place.

"Mom, did you ever know about the imagined house I had in the woods behind our summer cottage?" I asked my mother, as she lay in bed at the nursing home. I wanted to share these memories because her health was deteriorating fast.

"Sure," she said, "but I knew not to tell your sisters. That was such an important secret for you, and you needed to have an escape."

I smiled, surprised that my mother knew about my sojourn in the woods all these years, thankful that she had honored my need for independence.

"I was thinking about those woods the other day, feeling that my dream is being fulfilled," I told her. She nodded. She knew what I meant.

- - - - -

I wanted not just a house for my body. I wanted a house for my soul.

I gave thanks to this unique piece of heaven in a number of ways. To honor my body and soul, I gave up drinking alcohol. I did not want the daily struggle with alcohol to mar my relationship with this sacred place.

- - - - -

I surveyed the forested acres, cleared saplings and brush from the old farm road, and forged paths to the mountain streams.

I spent a week at the Ashram giving thanks for this opportunity to fulfill my Adirondack dream. To my enjoyment, the Ashram teachers gave us an assignment, a dharana:[66]

> Contemplate a place where you are protected and
> feel at peace. Take a journey there. Wallow in the
> sacred energy, the Shakti. Take this feeling back
> home with you.

The place that immediately surfaced as I did this contemplation was a spot by one of the mountain streams on my property—about a quarter-mile from the cleared field I was exploring as a site for a house, at the foot of the moraine where Nathan had meditated.

The moraine in the winter

I imagined walking to this sacred spot through the woods, down an embankment to the streambed, and sitting on a large rock by the stream, with the swift-flowing water cascading across the rocks in its path—all the while feeling protected by the forest canopy of white birches and balsam pines.

I imagined the water from the ground forming the stream that flows into Styles Brook, to the Ausable River, then Lake Champlain, then the St. Lawrence River, eventually becoming a part of the Atlantic Ocean. I felt the water flowing through my being as it advanced toward its many forms—from spring water in an aquifer to the vast waters of the ocean.

All I wanted to do was continue to honor this part of heaven, these Adirondack lands and waters.

Before the house was built, I camped out in the field to get a sense of the energy of this sacred land, and where a structure would best be placed on the three-acre open area. I wanted to cause as little disturbance as possible from the inevitable construction damage.

While researching alternative house design modalities, I found feng shui, the Chinese methodology and set of principles for living in harmony with the Chi, the universal energy.[67] The essence of home design using feng shui fit in with my years of meditating. I designed a home with the objective of supporting an uplifting, freeing existence—a home to complement my independent nature. I once again felt like a pioneer who had discovered and was able to apply the principles to enhance my search for my true nature.

The architect I selected also loved and respected the natural environment, appreciating my need to "walk softly on the earth." I wrote this note to her, explaining my hopes and dreams for this new abode:

> My wish is that this project and the resulting house and other amenities will be a continuation of what is already there—an area which is peaceful and walks quietly in its natural surroundings.
>
> I want the house to reflect the center of a spiritual retreat for Bruce and me and our guests. The house needs to be a comfortable home for me when I am alone, when Bruce is there, when our families visit, when our friends visit, and when we are not there.
>
> I expect that the process of building this house in the Adirondacks will be an uplifting experience. I want to take an active part and to work harmoniously with all involved in making our home in the Adirondacks a reality.

I asked that organic materials be used whenever possible by all the contractors, including low VOC paints and insulation, and natural materials of wood and stone. This was a challenge in the late '90s because the health problems caused by chemicals in our homes were just being recognized.

When trees needed to be cut, I hugged them, thanking them for providing sustenance for the earth.

I wanted to honor my childhood by incorporating elements of our cottage at Quaker Lake into the fray.

Camping in the field

"It's called 'novelty,' " the homeowner informed me after I stopped by to inquire about the wood siding on their colonial house. These were the same shingles we had on our cottage at Quaker, and I was having a hard time finding a match. I wanted to bring in the homey feel I had 50 years earlier as a child spending summers at the lake.

"I want an 'elegant' cottage feel to the design," I told my architect and builder. They succeeded with a 2100-square-foot, three-bedroom, two-bath home with a screen porch—and to the delight of all who visit, a sleeping porch. Great views of the Jay Mountain Wilderness and surrounding woods are visible through multiple windows in every room of the house. To help make up for the absence of a lake, we have a tiny pond, and a worn-out wooden sign above the front door, with faded red lettering saying, Welcome to the Lake.

We first built a garage with a high enough roof to accommodate a room with slanted ceilings—what we call the loft. I say "we" because Bruce finally recognized that his resistance to the Adirondacks was not bearing fruit, and he helped to finance the building of the house.

While it was being built, I felt like a pioneer as I camped out alone in the loft over the garage for six months. I say "camped out,"—I pitched a tent in the loft space to keep myself warm in the early spring and fall, since it was not insulated. I also pitched the tent to minimize the possibility of sleeping with the mice that roamed the garage and loft. The tent also kept away the mosquitoes while I read with the lights on.

One late afternoon following a rainstorm, I perched myself on a chair on the balcony of the loft, overlooking the mountains to the east. The sun from the west began shining through the moist air, causing a double rainbow to circle the sky over the mountains.

Rainbow over Jay Mountain.

Marveling at the sight, I whispered, "Mrs. Hawkins, here are our rainbows! The *somewhere* is this sacred place in the Adirondacks. All my years of aspiring to live a thriving, independent life, to discover my true nature and confront the challenges along the way have brought me to this place in my life."

I am blessed.

Epilogue

The other day I remembered an experience I had a few years ago meeting Gloria Steinem.

I mustered up my courage to approach her at the beginning of a Planned Parenthood event at the Mohawk Valley Country Club near Schenectady, New York, where she was the keynote speaker in December 2009.

Hoping I would have an opportunity to speak with Ms. Steinem, I assembled some of my early feminist literature to instantiate my credentials—that I was indeed part of the early women's movement.

I marched up to Gloria when there was a short line, introduced myself, and as I showed her the premier issue of *Ms. Magazine*, said, "Thank you for all you have done for women around the world, including me." She graciously nodded, and I continued, "We are of the same cohort, growing up in the '50s and '60s."

Gloria Steinem at the Planned Parenthood event

Gloria leaned toward me and said with a warm smile on her face, "We did it together—we survived the '50s."

I nodded, smiled, and thanked her again.

I came home enthralled with meeting such an accomplished woman, thinking, We did more than survive.

Gloria became the most accomplished feminist of the time as a freelance writer, journalist, and co-founder of *Ms. Magazine* and the National Women's Political Caucus. She flourished as a highly sought lecturer on women's issues, still commanding a faithful following on the speakers' circuit.

I survived the '50s in a more modest way. I overcame the limited expectations of women of this period, forging my way into a successful career while discovering a spiritual way of being. I learned how to thrive in my own way.

> Thriving is what was meant for us on this earth.
> Thriving, not just surviving, is our birthright as
> women.[68]

Acknowledgments

Throughout the process of writing this memoir, feelings of gratitude surfaced for all who supported me during the different phases of my life—my mother, Arvida Duvall; my husband of ten years, Dick Mead; my daughter, Jodi Mead; my partner of forty years, Bruce Berra; my teachers, friends, and professional colleagues. Their influence forms the matrix of my life. Some were players in this memoir, others not.

The pioneering efforts of women who led the feminist movement of the 1960s and 1970s deserve thanks for opening up choices for women. I felt their support as I struggled in my personal and professional dramas. The sharing of experiences in my consciousness-raising groups sustained my growth and gave me confidence to explore non-traditional paths.

My writing coach, David Hazard, helped to keep me moving toward a completed manuscript, providing encouragement and professional advice along the way. My early readers struggled through the first drafts, offering positive suggestions to clarify my intentions.

I am grateful for the kind and helpful guidance of Larry Gooley in molding this memoir into publishable form.

I thank them all.

> In the end, though, maybe we must all give up
> trying to pay back the people in this world who
> sustain our lives. In the end, maybe it's wiser to
> surrender before the miraculous scope of human
> generosity and to just keep saying thank you,
> forever and sincerely, for as long as we have
> voices.

—Elizabeth Gilbert. *Eat, Pray, Love.* p. 334.

Bibliography

Bianchi, Suzanne M. and Daphne Spain. *American Women in Transition*. New York: Russell Sage Foundation, 1986.

Boston Women's Health Book Collective. *Our Bodies, Ourselves*. Boston: New England Free Press, 1971.

Bosworth-Lingerfelt, Joyce. "Grief and Loss: A Part of the Japanese Experience". *Kansai Time Out*, February 1992, p. 10.

Chidvilasananda, Swami. *The Yoga of Discipline*. South Fallsburg, NY: SYDA Foundation, 1996.

Child, Julia and Louisette Bertholle, Simone Beck. *Mastering the Art of French Cooking*. New York: Alfred A. Knopf, 1966.

Dick-Read, Grantly. *Childbirth Without Fear: The Principles and Practice of Natural Childbirth*. London: Pinter & Martin, 1933.

Duvall, Lorraine M. *A Study of Problematic Situations and Information Needs of Software Managers in the United States and Japan*, CASE Center Technical Report No. 9321, Syracuse University, 1993.

Duvall, Lorraine M. *"A study of software management: the state of practice in the United States and Japan."* Journal of Systems and Software. Vol. 31 Issue 2, Nov. 1995 pp. 109–124.

Esko, Edward & Wendy. *Macrobiotic Cooking for Everyone*. Tokyo: Japan Publications, Inc., 1983.

Estes, Clarissa Pinkola. *Women Who Run With the Wolves*. New York: Random House, Inc., 1992.

Eykel, Kristen and Kathryn Arnold. *Yoga Journal and Lamaze present: Yoga for your pregnancy*. DVD, 2004.

Farb, Nathan. *The Adirondacks*. New York: Rizzoli, 1985.

Feuerstein, Georg. *The Yoga-Sutra of Patanjali*. Rochester, Vermont: Inner Traditions International, 1979.

Friedan, Betty. *The Feminist Mystique*. New York: Dell Publishing Co. Inc., 1964.

Friedan, Betty. *It Changed My Life: Writings on the Women's Movement*. Harvard University Press, 1998. Originally published, 1976.

Gilbert, Elizabeth. *Eat, Pray, Love*. London, England: Penguin Books Ltd., 2007.

Godfrey, Tim. *"The Japanese Dream of Flying." Kansai Time Out*, December 1991, p. 11.

Hanisch, Carol. *"The Personal is Political." Notes from the Second Year: Women's Liberation in 1970*.

Harragan, Betty Lehan, *Games Mother Never Taught You*. New York: Warner Books, Inc., 1977.

Heinemann, Sue. *Timelines of American Women's History*. Perigee Trade, 1996.

Imai, Masaaki. *Never take YES for an Answer*. Tokyo, Japan: The Simul Press, 1975.

Kamel, Marjorie. *Thank You, Dr. Lamaze: A Mother's Experiences in Painless Childbirth*. Philadelphia: J. B. Lippincott Company, 1959.

Kingston, Karen. *Creating Sacred Space with Feng Shui*. New York: Broadway Books, 1997.

Kripananda, Swami. *Jnaneshwar's Gita: A Rendering of the Jnaneshwari: Bhagavad Gita*. South Fallsburg, NY: SYDA Foundation, 1999.

LaBastille, Anne. *Woodswoman*. New York: E.P. Dutton, 1978.

Leomard, Vince. "Miss USA: Real Name's Barbara." *Pittsburgh Press*, 13 May 1965.

Lopate, Phillip. *To Show and To Tell: The Craft of Literary Nonfiction.* New York: Free Press, 2013.

Lucy Kamisar. *"The New Feminism,"* Saturday Review, February 21, 1970.

Marciniak, John J., Editor. *Encyclopedia of Software Engineering.* New York: John Wiley & Sons, Inc., 1994, Vol. 1, p. 438.

Muktananda, Swami. *Play of Consciousness.* Oakland, CA: SYDA Foundation, 1978.

Prakash, Prem. *The Yoga of Spiritual Devotion: A Modern Translation of the Narada Bhakti Sutras.* Inner Traditions, 1998.

Reben, Martha. *The Healing Woods.* New York: Thomas Y. Crowell Company, 1952.

Riccardo, J. J., President, Chrysler Corporation. *"Women's Reluctance to Move Ahead… And How It Can Be Overcome"* Reprinted from the *Detroit Free Press* in a series on federal Revised Order 4 and its effect on women, business, and industry.

Ricci, Isolina. *Mom's House, Dad's House: Making Shared Custody Work.* New York: Collier Books, 1980.

Sing the Name: The Meaning and Significance of Thirty-Six Devotional Chants. SYDA Foundation 1997. p. 33.

Singh, Jaideva. *Siva Sutras: The Yoga of Supreme Identity.* Delhi, India: Motilal Banarsidass, 1979.

Steinem, Gloria. *Revolution from Within: A Book of Self-Esteem.* Boston: Little, Brown and Company, 1992.

Weber, Sandra and Peggy Lynn. *Breaking Trail: Remarkable Women of the Adirondacks*. Purple Mountain Press, Ltd., 2004.

Williams, W. W. "No Vague Dream." *Kansai Time Out*, February 1992, p. 8.

Winter, Kate H. *The Woman in the Mountain: Reconstructions of Self and Land by Adirondack Women Writers*. Albany: State University of New York Press, 1989.

End Notes

1.   Jay Leibold, *Fight for Freedom,* Random House Children's Books, 1990.

2.   A *tip sheet* from a1949 Singer sewing machine manual advised women "to never try to sew with a sink full of dishes or beds unmade ... make yourself as attractive as possible ... put on a clean dress ... have your hair in order, powder and lipstick put on with care. If you are constantly fearful that a visitor would drop in or your husband will come home and you will not look neatly put together, you will not enjoy your sewing as you should."

3.   Scarlet O'Neil was the first super-powered female character to appear in comic form, making her debut in 1940 in the *Chicago Times.* Scarlet O'Neil only possessed one super power: invisibility. She acquired this ability as a young girl, curiously, by putting her finger into a weird-looking ray of light emanating from one of her father's experiments. After a while, Scarlet discovered that she could become invisible or visible by pressing a highly sensitive nerve on her left wrist.

Figures of Scarlet and other characters from her adventures were available as paper doll cutouts and unpainted plaster figures.

Trina Robbins, author of *The Great Women Superheroes,* stated in an interview for *The Untold Origins of Invisible Scarlet O'Neil* book, "The 1940s was a great time for strong women characters in comics, as it was for real-life women. The country was at war, and while the men were overseas, women stepped in to fill their jobs, doing things women had never done before: driving trucks and buses, making ships and planes, even flying the planes, and this new 'We can do it' attitude was reflected in comics. Then the boys came home and wanted their old jobs back, and the mood of the country changed. Suddenly women were encouraged to marry, start families, and stay home. Again, this was reflected in comics, and the image of strong women disappeared for over 30 years."

4.   In 1954 the only way to treat cancer was to surgically remove the tumor, if possible. Half of my father's stomach was removed. However, as the cancer had spread to his esophagus tube, there was nothing they could do to stop the spread. The use of chemotherapy to kill cancer cells was in the early research stage. Radiation was used sparingly since the large doses used then were known to cause more cancer.

5.	In 1957, 95 percent of doctors, lawyers, and scientists were men, The National Manpower Commission. From *American Women in Transition*, p. 128. An interesting study on specific jobs held by men and women presented U.S. Employment Service data showing that between 1959 and 1979, the vast majority of women workers' job titles were different than a man's, illustrating the job segregation of the times. pp. 164–65

6.	The median annual salary for women in 1960 was $3,257: $5,368 for men. *American Women in Transition*. p. 170.

7.	The median age for first marriages in 1964 was 20 for women; 22 for men. Only 10 percent of women in the 25-to-29 age range had never married.

8.	*"... we even foresee the day when a family will relocate its household because of a change in employment of the wife instead of the husband."* Gloria Steinem addressing this issue at the first Women's Rights Meeting sponsored by the YWCA of Metropolitan Chicago February 16, 1972. This happened with my daughter's family when she took a tenured track position in the math department at Boise State University in 2000.

9.	Couples in the academic sciences are beginning to address "The Two Body Problem" as more women earn science degrees. http://www.physics.wm.edu/~sher/dualcareer.html.

10.	The federal Equal Credit Opportunity Act, enacted in 1974, makes it unlawful for any creditor to discriminate against any applicant with respect to any aspect of a credit transaction, on the basis of race, color, religion, national origin, sex, marital status, or age. The Chicago Chapter of NOW was instrumental in the passage of an Illinois fair credit law.

11.	The Pregnancy Discrimination Act of 1978 amended Title VII of the Civil Rights Act of 1964, stating that an employer may not single out pregnancy-related conditions to determine an employee's ability to work.
	In 1991, AT&T paid a record $66 million to settle a 1978 discrimination complaint filed with the EEOC by employees who were forced to go on unpaid leave when they were six or seven months pregnant. *Timelines of American Women's History*, p. 138.

12.	The natural birthing views emanated from the book by Dick-Read, *Childbirth Without Fear*, who believed that fear of childbirth could be eliminated by educating women.

13. The Lamaze method of painless childbirth consists of two basic principles: 1) an all-encompassing education of the mother on the birthing process and, 2) the development of conditioned reflexes to help in the process. It is a modification of the Russian Pavlov method, call psycho-prophylaxis, i.e., the use of psychological and physical conditioning.

14. The Appendix contained the *Manual of Information and Practical Exercises for Painless Childbirth* by Mmes. Rennert & Cohen, Karmel's nurses in Paris.

15. A 2004 DVD highlights the techniques related to classic yoga, *Yoga Journal and Lamaze present: Yoga for your pregnancy*.

16. A groundbreaking book published in 1971 by a group of feminists boldly, for the first time, spoke of women's health issues, including childbirth—three years after my daughter was born. Reference: *Our Bodies, Ourselves*, Boston Womens' Health Course Collective, 1971.

17. I was part of the team when my grandson was born 30 years later. My son-in-law attended Lamaze classes with my daughter and was in the delivery room, coaching her along. I felt honored when my daughter asked me to be a part of the team. A nurse included me in the birth process by saying, "Hey Grandma, take that washcloth, soak it with cold water, and put it to the new mother's lips to help quench her thirst." After the delivery, my daughter also wanted something to eat, just like Marjorie Karmel did after the birth of her second child using the Lamaze method.

18. The Human Potential Movement built upon the philosophies of Fritz Perl, Carl Rogers, and Abraham Maslow to develop techniques for sensitivity training and group therapy. See http://www.pathacross. com/human-potential-movement.

19. New York, premier issue of *Ms. Magazine*, December 1971; "The Politics of Housework" by Pat Mainardi; "The Spokeswoman" 1971–1973; *Our Bodies, Ourselves*, Boston Women' Health Course Collective, 1971; National Organization for Women Newsletters, 1971–1972.

20. A seminal article on "The Politics of Housework", originally published by Pat Mainardi of Redstockings in 1970 and reprinted in the first issue of *Ms. Magazine*, speaks of all the ways men trivialize housework to try to rid themselves of any responsibility. She writes how her

husband "proceeded to change from a normally sweet, considerate Dr. Jekyll into the crafty Mr. Hyde who would stop at nothing to avoid the horrors of housework."

21. "The 1973 NOW annual convention closed with the playing of 'I Am Woman.' "Suddenly, women got out of their seats and started dancing around the hotel ballroom and joining hands in a circle that got larger and larger until maybe a thousand of us were dancing and singing, 'I am strong, I am invincible, I am woman.' It was a spontaneous, beautiful expression of the exhilaration we all felt in those years, women really moving as women." Betty Friedan from *It Changed My Life*, p. 257.

22. Consciousness-Raising Groups in the late 1960s and early '70s brought women together to explore their common needs in achieving equality in their lives personally, professionally, and educationally. Small CR Groups were the backbone of the feminist movement, destroying the isolation women experienced in a male-dominated society.

23. No-fault divorce is a divorce in which the dissolution of a marriage does not require a showing of wrongdoing by either party. In 1970, California adopted the nation's first no-fault divorce law. By 2010, all 50 states had legalized no-fault divorce.

24. Joint-custody encompasses both legal and physical aspects. Legal custody refers to the parental right to make major decisions regarding the child's health, education, and welfare. Physical custody refers to the living arrangements of the child on a day-to-day basis. In 1979, California was the first state to enact a joint-custody statute. By 1991 most states had recognized the concept of joint custody in case law.

25. In 1968, 20 percent of husbands requested custody. By 1972, that percentage was down to 13, and in 1977 it had slipped to 7.8. By 1977, 63 percent of the fathers who requested custody received it.

26. *Mom's House, Dad's House: Making Shared Custody Work*. Isolina Ricci. Collier Books, 1980.

27. March 25, 1960. A note written to me by my Professor of Mental Hygiene at Grove City College responding to my paper for an assignment of essays on famous quotations.

28.   *"How to start your own consciousness-raising group."* Guidelines from a 1971 leaflet written by the Chicago Women's Liberation Union.

29.   *Our Bodies Our Selves: A Course by and for Women,* Published by the Boston Women's Health Course Collective, addressed women's health issues not available to the lay public. I bought a copy from the second printing: April 1971. As stated in the Forward, "The first printing sold so fast we haven't had time to revise the printed course. We are working on revisions which we hope will be ready for the 3rd printing." This landmark book is one of 88 books included in the 2012 Library of Congress exhibition, "Books that Shaped America," a list of important works "intended to spark a national conversation on books written by Americans that have influenced our lives." www.ourbodiesourselves.org.

30.   Carol Hanisch said that consciousness-raising worked because it destroyed the isolation that men used to maintain their authority and supremacy. She explained in her famous essay *"The Personal is Political"* that consciousness-raising groups were not a psychological therapy group but rather a valid form of political action, that coming to a personal realization of how "grim" the situation was, for them was as important as doing political action, such as protests.
Lucy Kamisar stated it a little differently: "… a kind of group therapy or encounter session that starts with the premise that there is something wrong with the system, not the women in the group." From *"The New Feminism," Saturday Review*, February 21, 1970.

31.   Gloria Steinem, *Revolution from Within*, p. 323.

32.   GE was the leading contractor for the Air Force for strategic missile re-entry vehicles. As early as 1956, GE's Richard Porter had done pioneering work for the US Air Force in solving the re-entry capsule problem, culminating in the enormous Mark 6 re-entry vehicle for the 3175 kg Titan II warhead.

33.   In 1968, the Equal Employment Opportunity Commission banned all help-wanted ads that specified the preferred sex of the applicant, except those jobs where sex was a bona-fide occupational requirement (such as actress).

34.   "Miss USA: Real Name's Barbara" by Vince Leomard. *Pittsburgh Press.* 13 May 1965.

35. Gender discrimination in places of public accommodation is largely left to the states. The US did not include sex as a protected class in Title II of the 1964 Civil Rights Act, which is the federal public accommodations law.

    In 1969 the National Organization for Women picketed men-only restaurants and bars in New York City. Subsequently in a case filed by two NOW activist lawyers, the NY Supreme Court ruled that the men-only policy of McSorley's Olde Ale House, a public restaurant in New York City, was illegal. New York City in 1970 passed a law prohibiting sex discrimination in most public facilities—the first such law in a major city.

36. Carol Kleiman, a columnist for the *Chicago Tribune*, wrote in the early '70s about how women need more options to the 9 p.m. to 5 p.m. work schedule. She asks, "Why not a tandem team of two women for each job, each working on a four-hour shift? Or, why not a five-hour day? Or why not a three-day week? Or why not *some* flexibility in hours for mothers of young children?" Questions still relevant today, in 2014.

    Catalyst, a social activist organization formed in 1962, focused its efforts in 1970 on the benefits of part-time work for women. www. catalyst.org.

37. In September 1972, I wrote a letter to Catalyst's headquarters in New York, stating: "I am presently working as a computer analyst on a part-time basis in Chicago. I work a 5-day week, 6 hours a day on a regular basis, but am still considered a temporary worker and receive no benefits. I love the job and the schedule works fine with my other roles of wife and mother. I am beginning to put together a case for my management to change their stringent definitions for a permanent employee (40 hours per week). I would appreciate any inputs you may have." Unfortunately, I never received a reply.

38. In 1969, white females received 58 percent of the income received by white males, on average. This is in contrast to 47 percent for non-white females. Non-white females received 70 percent of the income received by non-white males. *Women in Transition.* pp. 178–179.

39. Full Affirmative Action rights were expanded in a 1967 Executive Order to cover discrimination based on sex. Federal agencies and contractors were required to take active measures to ensure women and minorities access to educational and employment opportunities equal to white males.

40. *"Women's Reluctance to Move Ahead ... And How It Can Be Overcome"* by J. J. Riccardo, President, Chrysler Corporation. Reprinted from the *Detroit Free Press* in a series on federal Revised Order 4 and its effect on women, business, and industry.

41. In 1963 President Kennedy signed the Equal Pay Act into law, which amended the Fair Labor Standards Act to prohibit pay discrimination because of sex. However, even in 2013, women are consistently paid less than men for the same job.

42. The Equal Rights Amendment (ERA) was a proposed amendment to the US Constitution designed to guarantee equal rights for women. In 1972, it passed both houses of Congress and went to the state legislatures for ratification, needing 38 of the 50 states, but fell 3 short of becoming a part of the Constitution.

43. Beginning in 1977, NOW encouraged the economic boycott of unratified states by refusing to attend or hold conventions in targeted states. This initiative caused states to lose millions of dollars and was supported by dozens of organizations including the League of Women Voters and the United Auto Workers.

44. "Association for Women in Computing Formed," *Computerworld.* December 18, 1978.
     The AWC continues as a networking organization for women. See http://www.awc-hq.org. "We are a national professional organization for professionals involved with information and technology dedicated to the advancement of women in the technology fields. We offer camaraderie with like-minded professionals through our chapters and a growing network of independent members." From the 2013 website. The process of forming the AWC was similar to how NOW came into being. A group of women attending the third National Conference of State Commissions on the Status of Women held in 1966 were dissatisfied when the conference organizers did not allow resolutions or actions of any kind meant to abolish discrimination against women. Betty Friedan and other women attending the conference put their five dollars on the table and formed the National Organization for Women (NOW).

45. Artificial Intelligence techniques can help in predicting the severity of a power outage and developing contingency plans, for example.

46. The US Department of Defense initiated an effort in the late '70s and early '80s to encourage the use of the Ada Programming Language in new software engineering efforts. To this end we developed the concept of, designed, and implemented the Ada Information Clearinghouse, which is still in existence. See www.adaic.org.

47. Betty Lehan Harragan in her 1977 book *Games Mother Never Taught You* writes that women were in an "alien culture," operating from a different perspective than men. She asserts that success is contingent on a key strategy "to make accurate predictions of your opponent's move, then outwitting them at their own game." p. 44.

48. Teachings came from the Bhagavad Gita, Yoga Sutras, the Bhakti Sutras, the Siva Sutras.

49. The primordial sounds of the ancient Sanskrit language are the natural progression of vibration as created in the human vocal cords.

50. Immersing oneself in a chant washes away impurities of the past. Swami Chidvilasananda, *The Yoga of Discipline*, pg. 90.

51. On November 18, 1978, 918 people died in Jonestown, Guyana, at the settlement for the Peoples Temple, led by Jim Jones. It was a socialist paradise, described by Jones as a benevolent communist community. The deaths of the members of the settlement were caused by murder and suicide by drinking cyanide poisoning.

52. These old patterns are called *samskaras* in the Sanskrit language, stored impressions from a previous thought or action held within the subtle body. Everything we do and think and feel is recorded.

53. *Siva Sutra Pravesana: An Introduction for Practitioners of Yoga*. Paul E. Muller-Ortega, Ph.D. 2009.

54. This transmission of spiritual energy from an enlightened being to the student is called Shaktipat in Sanskrit, an initiation into a higher level of consciousness.

55. I had received Shaktipat from Baba, an awakening of the spiritual energy, the Kundalini Shakti.

56. The Bhakti Sutras is an ancient text from the sage Narada that details the way of devotion, bhakti, to achieve oneness to the divine consciousness.

57. The year was 1987. Strict security procedures in airports had not yet been instituted. No photo identification was required. Visitors could meet passengers at the airport gates. The terrorist attack—with bombs placed on Pan Am flight 103 and the resultant explosion over Lockerby, Scotland, killing all 259 people on board and an additional 11 people on the ground—had not yet occurred.

58. One hundred eighty-nine Americans died on December 21, 1988, as a result of a bomb exploding on Pan Am 103, with the fiery plane crashing into the town of Lockerby, Scotland.

59. John J. Marciniak, Editor, *Encyclopedia of Software Engineering* (John Wiley & Sons, Inc., 1994), Vol. 1, p. 438.

60. The research opportunity in Japan enriched my dissertation, resulting in the awarding of my Ph.D. in 1993. See, Lorraine M. Duvall, *A Study of Problematic Situations and Information Needs of Software Managers in the United States and Japan*, CASE Center Technical Report No. 9321, Syracuse University, 1993.

61. Koji chaired a software-engineering laboratory at Osaka University, fondly known internationally as Torii-Lab. Kishida, as president of a small Japanese software development company, Software Research Associates (SRA), often sponsored research contracts at Torii-Lab.

62. "No Vague Dream" by W.W. Williams, *Kansai Time Out*, February 1992, p. 8.

63. "The Japanese Dream of Flying" by Tim Godfrey. *Kansai Time Out*, December 1991, p. 11.

64. "Grief and Loss: A Part of the Japanese Experience" by Joyce Bosworth–Lingerfelt, *Kansai Time Out*, February 1992, p. 10.

65. In later years, two books directly addressed the independence of Adirondack women: *The Woman in the Mountain* by Kate Winter and *Breaking Trail: Remarkable Women of the Adirondacks* by Sandra Weber and Peggy Lynn.

66. A dharana is concentration on an object, a situation. Its purpose is to empty the mind to heal, to help see the way clearly and to recognize one's dharma, duty, path to follow—to live in line with one's own divine will.

67. I attended courses and read a vast amount of literature to help in applying this body of knowledge to my building project. *Creating Sacred Space with Feng Shui* by Karen Kingston provides a good introduction to feng shui as practiced in the West.

68. *Women Who Run With the Wolves*, Clarissa Pinkola Estes, p. 198.